50 Ways For A Start Up to Raise Investment Using Chat GPT

The Grumpy Entrepreneur

Published by The Grumpy Entrepreneur, 2023.

While every precaution has been taken in the preparation of this book, the publisher assumes no responsibility for errors or omissions, or for damages resulting from the use of the information contained herein.

50 WAYS FOR A START UP TO RAISE INVESTMENT USING CHAT GPT

First edition. September 15, 2023.

ISBN: 979-8223261735

Written by The Grumpy Entrepreneur.

Always for my girls Trina, Harriet and Georgina

My family!

For all those who have supported me in my startup journey

My good mate Kevin Doyle who started me on the first part of my journey and beyond.

My great lawyer Tom Cottrell has supported me massively in the last few challenging months.

50 Ways for a Startup to Raise Investment Using ChatGPT

By David Murray-Hundley "The Grumpy Entrepreneur"

Contents

Forward

Ask any entrepreneur , there biggest challenges its probably been raising investment or getting those first sales. Its then followed by how time consuming raising investment is and how it can effect whole aspects of the day to day stuff.

So whilst I have written this with ChatGPT in mind, I would still lazy, dont think this is the answer to everything. Still needs human interaction.

I thought I would start with some tips below and who should read this. I could write a lot more but frankly every good entrepreneur will want to find out for themselves. Enjoy.

Key Points:

Raising Too Much or Too Little Money: Striking the right balance between raising too much or too little money is critical. While not having enough money might result in the business going under, raising too much puts undue pressure from investors for immediate performance.

Giving Up Too Much Of The Company: Entrepreneurs should be careful not to give away a large stake in their company as it may cost them more in the long run, impacting control and decision-making.

Having No Plan For Scaling: A well-thought-out scaling plan is essential when looking for investors. This includes having a robust infrastructure with systems, procedures, and physical space to accommodate growth.

Raising Funds Too Early: The timing of the fundraise is essential. Startups should not rush into fundraising without validating their business model and having a solid foundation.

Failing To Research Investors: Knowing the investor's portfolio and their investment strategies can significantly improve a startup's chances of getting funded.

Being Underprepared: Entrepreneurs often underestimate the time and effort required for fundraising. It's crucial to have a well-prepared pitch deck and be ready to answer tough questions convincingly.

Ignoring The Need For A Contingency Plan: It's beneficial to have alternative plans in case negotiations with potential investors fall through. This can provide leverage during discussions.

Asking For Investment At First Interaction: Building a relationship with potential investors before asking for money increases the likelihood of a successful investment.

Not Asking For Enough: Don't undercut the amount needed for the startup to function successfully. Be bold, but realistic, about the money you need and be prepared to back it up with data.

Not Seeking Professional Advice: Given the complexities involved, seeking professional advice from mentors or financial advisors can prove invaluable.

Who Should Read This:

• Startup Entrepreneurs: This book is a must-read for startup founders, especially those who are navigating the world of fundraising for the first time.

• Investors: Investors can benefit from understanding the mistakes entrepreneurs commonly make, helping them make better investment decisions.

• Business Consultants and Advisors: They can use this as a guide to counsel their clients on best practices for fundraising.

Chapter 1: Drafting the Perfect Elevator Pitch

The elevator pitch. The high-stakes, 30-second monologue that can make or break your dream project in those 30 seconds. Imagine stepping into an elevator, and there stands the one investor who can turn your garage startup into the next tech sensation. Your heart races, palms sweat, but wait—you've got your elevator pitch ready to go, and it's a masterpiece.It might seem something like the movies but I have heard furst hand from people that have taken the moment and raised in some crazy places

Why It Matters

IN A WORLD BUZZING with noise, where attention spans are shorter than a goldfish's memory (no offense to goldfish), a concise, compelling elevator pitch is your golden ticket to Investor Land. It's your 30-second spotlight, the verbal equivalent of a first impression—and we all know how much those count.By the way I expect this to change again in the next few years with AI being used more.

What Makes a Pitch Perfect?

A PITCH-PERFECT ELEVATOR pitch is the beautiful offspring of simplicity and specificity. It should capture the essence of your business idea while making the listener lean in and say, "Tell me more."Its also for someone like me whether personally or through Pario Ventures.

The Formula

THE SECRET FORMULA for a killer elevator pitch is simple: Problem + Solution + Market + Traction. The order isn't set in stone, but the elements are non-negotiable.

Problem: What issue are you solving?

Solution: How are you solving it?

Market: Who will pay for it?

Traction: Why should they believe you can pull it off?

ChatGPT to the Rescue

HERE'S WHERE CHATGPT shines like a knight in pixelated armor. By generating various permutations and combinations of these four elements, you can fine-tune your pitch to crystal clarity. Just feed in the essential details and voilà—you've got yourself an array of pitch options faster than you can say "seed funding."

Real-world Example

LET'S IMAGINE YOUR startup is about using AI to help farmers optimize crop yields.

Bad Pitch: "We use machine learning algorithms to analyze complex data sets for farmers."

Good Pitch with ChatGPT: "We help farmers increase profits by 30% using AI to tell them exactly when to water, feed, and harvest their crops. With a $100 billion market and a pilot project already succeeding, we're the future of agriculture."

See the difference? The second pitch is compelling, concise, and oozes credibility.

Final Touches

THE FINAL SPRINKLE of magic in any elevator pitch is your delivery. ChatGPT can't hold your hand and make you sound like Morgan Freeman, but it can help you practice by generating a variety of questions an investor might ask after hearing your pitch.

In wrapping up this chapter, it's clear that the versatility of ChatGPT in creating dynamic and effective elevator pitches can be likened to having a personal speechwriter and business strategist rolled into one. Now, let's pivot towards some actionable tips that you can start applying today.

Tip 1: Always A/B Test

USE CHATGPT TO DRAFT multiple versions of your elevator pitch. Present these to a small group of trusted business colleagues or friends and gather feedback. This way, you can quickly determine which pitch is more effective before meeting a potential investor.

Tip 2: Spice it up with Statistics

A WELL-PLACED STATISTIC can amplify your pitch's impact. Use ChatGPT's data summarization capabilities to extract compelling statistics related to your business sector and incorporate them seamlessly into your pitch.

Tip 3: Keep the Conversation Going

AN ELEVATOR PITCH SHOULD not be the end but the beginning of a dialogue. Use ChatGPT to also draft engaging follow-up questions that can help deepen the discussion post-pitch, such as "What's your take on sustainable agriculture?" or "How important is data security in your business?"

Your elevator pitch is often the first impression you'll make on potential investors. With the help of ChatGPT, not only can you make it a good one, but you can also lay the foundation for future conversations that could steer your business towards unprecedented growth. Ready to elevate your pitch game to the next level? Don't miss the upcoming chapters for more ways to captivate your audience and secure that investment.

Chapter 2: Automated Market Research Summaries

M arket research, the kale of the business world. Everyone knows it's good for you, but not everyone wants to chew through it. Let's face it, combing through endless spreadsheets, customer surveys, and market analyses feels about as exciting as watching paint dry on a humid day. But what if I told you ChatGPT could whip up a kale smoothie so delicious you'd forget you're consuming something healthy?

The 'Why Bother?' Factor

INVESTORS ARE SHARP-eyed creatures who feast on data. If your startup were a movie, your elevator pitch would be the trailer, but your market research is the full-length feature. It shows you've done your homework and, more importantly, that there's a real-world audience for your product.

Recipe for a Data Smoothie

A WELL-CRAFTED MARKET research summary needs a pinch of this and a dash of that—customer demographics, market size, growth potential, competitors, and so on. Sounds exhausting, right? But here's where ChatGPT, your personal data chef, comes into play.

The ChatGPT Twist

JUST AS YOU WOULDN'T shove an entire salad into a blender and hope for the best, don't expect ChatGPT to do all the heavy lifting without some quality ingredients. Feed it well-researched data, and watch it concoct a compelling narrative that even the most skeptical investor can't resist.

Simply input your raw data and ask something like, "Summarize this market research in a way that highlights the growth potential of my startup." ChatGPT will turn that raw information into a cocktail of insights, aperitifs of trends, and a dessert of actionable strategies.

Real-world Example

IMAGINE YOU'RE VENTURING into the eco-friendly toothbrush market which my the way is not a easy product to selll to consumers.

Bad Summary: "Eco-friendly toothbrushes are popular. Many companies are doing it. We should too."

Good Summary with ChatGPT: "The eco-friendly toothbrush market is exploding, projected to grow at a CAGR of 15% over the next five years. While established players focus on adult markets, our research shows an untapped potential in the pediatric segment. With our patented bamboo design and early talks with dental clinics, we're poised to bite off a significant market share."

Notice how the ChatGPT version gives depth, context, and paints a picture of opportunity? It's like comparing a summer blockbuster to a low-budget YouTube sketch.

The Final Stir

AS WE CLOSE THIS CHAPTER, one thing becomes abundantly clear: ChatGPT can revolutionize the way you conduct and summarize market research. The process is not just automated but also significantly more insightful, thanks to AI's ability to analyze and understand context. Here are some targeted tips to help you get the most out of your automated market research summaries.

Tip 1: Prioritize Key Metrics

BEFORE YOU TASK CHATGPT with generating a market research summary, identify the key metrics or KPIs (Key Performance Indicators) that are most relevant to your business. Feed these metrics into the AI to ensure that your summary is tightly focused and provides actionable insights.

Tip 2: Cross-reference Data Points

USE CHATGPT TO COMPILE summaries from multiple sources. Cross-referencing data this way provides a more balanced and comprehensive view of the market landscape. Plus, it can highlight any inconsistencies that warrant further investigation.

Tip 3: Keep it Dynamic

MARKETS CHANGE, AND so should your research. Make it a habit to use ChatGPT for generating updated market research summaries on a regular basis, whether quarterly, monthly, or even weekly. This will ensure that your strategies and approaches remain relevant and effective.

The advent of ChatGPT brings us one step closer to making comprehensive, yet concise market research a regular part of the entrepreneurial toolbox. Your time can now be better spent on strategizing and implementing, leaving the laborious task of data summarization to your ever-efficient AI assistant.

Chapter 3: Generating Investment Proposals

Investment proposal: the red carpet that leads to the sparkling ballroom of investor relations. Or, if you mess it up, the banana peel that has you sliding straight into the "no" pile. The stakes are high, but fear not. ChatGPT is here, armed with a digital pen and an arsenal of tips to turn your investment proposal into an offer no one can refuse.

The 'Let's Get Serious' Moment

THE ELEVATOR PITCH gets you through the door, and the market research shows you've got your head on straight. But the investment proposal? That's the wedding ring, the lifelong commitment that says you're worth the investment and on the road to maybe making the investor some money. In this document, you'll dive into financials, strategies, and projections—the meat and potatoes of why anyone should give you money.

The Ingredients

CREATING AN INVESTMENT proposal is much like assembling a complex Lego castle which needs lots of patience. You have various pieces like the executive summary, market analysis, financial projections, exit strategy, and so forth. Leaving out one could mean the difference between a solid fortress and a crumbling mess.

The ChatGPT Touch

NOW, WOULDN'T IT BE grand if you had a trusty squire to sort through these Lego pieces, ensuring they fit just right? Enter

ChatGPT. Once you have your primary research and main ideas jotted down, you can have ChatGPT help flesh out each section.

Ask for help with phrases like, "ChatGPT, can you write an executive summary focusing on the unique technology of my startup?" or "Generate a description of my startup's growth strategy based on these key points." The AI whizzes into action, generating content as precise and smooth as a latte from your favorite hipster cafe.

Real-world Example

SUPPOSE YOU'RE LAUNCHING a startup that provides affordable solar energy solutions for remote communities.

Bad Proposal: "We want to sell solar panels to people in far-off places. Give us money, and we'll figure it out."

Good Proposal with ChatGPT: "Our venture aims to democratize energy access, targeting remote communities with affordable, easy-to-install solar panel kits. With a total addressable market of $5 billion and a pilot program already impacting 1,000 households, we're seeking $2 million in Series A funding to scale our operations and empower communities worldwide."

Notice the second proposal speaks the investor's language—clear, quantifiable, and with a hint of world-changing ambition.

The Cherry on Top

AS WE WRAP UP THIS chapter on generating investment proposals with ChatGPT, it's hard not to marvel at how AI has transformed this once arduous task into something more efficient and nuanced. Your proposals can now be tailored to each investor, capturing not just the figures but also the vision behind your venture. Let's delve into some expert tips to fine-tune this process even further.

Tip 1: Tell a Story

REMEMBER THAT NUMBERS alone don't make an investment compelling; the story does. Use ChatGPT to help you craft a narrative around your financials, bringing life to balance sheets and cash flow statements.

Tip 2: Be Transparent

TRANSPARENCY IS KEY in any investment proposal. Utilize ChatGPT to create appendices or additional sections that transparently outline risks, assumptions, and mitigation plans. This adds layers of trust and credibility to your proposal.

Tip 3: Personalize, Personalize, Personalize

USE CHATGPT'S CUSTOMIZATION capabilities to tailor your investment proposals to each investor. Highlight aspects that would most appeal to them, whether it's sustainability, rapid scalability, or long-term profitability.

With ChatGPT at your disposal, generating investment proposals doesn't have to be a time-consuming chore. It can be an opportunity to shine, to convey your business acumen and vision in a document that stands out in a sea of generic pitches. You're not just asking for money; you're inviting a partnership built on vision, trust, and mutual benefit. So, as we close this chapter, consider this: Are you ready to redefine the investment proposal game?

Chapter 4: Creating a Dynamic Business Plan

B usiness plan—perhaps the most misunderstood document in the startup universe. Some think of it as a relic, a dusty old tome that once had relevance. But savvy entrepreneurs—and ChatGPT—know better. A business plan is your startup's North Star, a dynamic blueprint that not only guides your journey but sells it to others.Its also what might catch you out in thefuture

The 'Business Bible' You Can't Ignore

A BUSINESS PLAN ISN'T just another checkbox on your startup to-do list; it's your comprehensive guide to startup stardom. Think of it as the script for a blockbuster movie. It tells everyone involved—founders, employees, investors—what roles they play, what scenes need to unfold, and most importantly, why this movie is a must-see.

What's in a Plan?

A GREAT BUSINESS PLAN is like a hearty stew, simmering with various ingredients that come together to create a sumptuous whole. You've got your executive summary, market analysis, organization and management details, service or product line description, sales strategies, funding requests, and financial projections. That's a lot of potatoes to peel!

ChatGPT's Secret Sauce

GENERATING A BUSINESS plan from scratch can be intimidating, but ChatGPT can be your trusty sous-chef. It can whip up appetizing sections of your business plan that not only meet formal criteria but also sparkle with entrepreneurial flair.

You might request, "ChatGPT, help me outline the marketing strategy for my organic juice bar," or "Provide me with a risk analysis for my e-commerce fashion startup." Just like that, ChatGPT will serve you delicious morsels of text, ready to be added to your stew.

Real-world Example

LET'S SAY YOU'RE PIONEERING a mobile app that connects local artisans with art lovers in their community.

Bad Business Plan: "We're creating an app for artists. There are artists everywhere. This will be big!"

Good Business Plan with ChatGPT: "Our mobile app aims to revolutionize local art scenes by connecting artisans directly with art enthusiasts. With an addressable market of 40 million art buyers in the U.S alone, our platform offers features like virtual galleries, AI-curated selections, and secure transaction methods. We anticipate 20% user growth in the first year with a multi-phase marketing strategy, including influencer partnerships and targeted social media campaigns."

Now, isn't that a plan you'd want to invest in?

The Finishing Touches

AS WE CONCLUDE THIS chapter on creating dynamic business plans with ChatGPT, it becomes increasingly evident how indispensable AI can be for modern entrepreneurs. Not only can you generate comprehensive business plans with ease, but you can also adapt them quickly to changing market conditions. Below are a few tips to make this process even smoother:

Tip 1: Use Scenario Analysis

EMPLOY CHATGPT TO DEVELOP various business scenarios, from best-case to worst-case. A dynamic business plan should account for multiple possible futures, equipping you to pivot as needed.

Tip 2: Keep It Living

TRADITIONAL BUSINESS plans often sit in a drawer collecting dust. Not yours. Use ChatGPT to update your business plan regularly, adapting to new insights, market conditions, and opportunities.

Tip 3: Seek External Feedback

WHILE CHATGPT CAN GENERATE a fantastic business plan, it can't replace human feedback. Use the AI-generated plan as a starting point, then seek advice from trusted mentors or industry experts to refine it further.

With ChatGPT in your entrepreneurial toolkit, gone are the days of static, cumbersome business plans. You now have a dynamic document that evolves with your business, providing a continually updated roadmap to success. No longer a one-time effort but an ongoing strategy, your business plan can become the living document that it was always meant to be

Chapter 5: Crafting the Perfect Investor Presentation

A h, the investor presentation: the Broadway show of the entrepreneurial world. The stage is set, the audience is seated, and it's your moment to shine. Forget the spotlight; we're talking full-beam projectors displaying your life's work in a series of slides. The question is, will your performance result in a standing ovation or polite golf claps?

Setting the Scene

IMAGINE WALKING INTO a conference room with investors eyeing you like Simon Cowell eyes talent show contestants. You have their attention but haven't yet won their hearts. You plug in your laptop, take a deep breath, and launch your presentation. This is your movie trailer, executive summary, business plan, and charm all rolled into one electrifying package.

Slide into Success

A STELLAR INVESTOR presentation features a medley of slides, each more captivating than the last—problem statement, solution, market size, business model, and so on. But, oh, the horror of seeing eyes glaze over as you flick through monotonous slides brimming with text!

ChatGPT: The Ghostwriter of Wall Street

WHILE CHATGPT MAY NOT have design chops, it does possess a particular set of skills—skills acquired over extensive training. Skills that make it a dream for people like you. Just tell it what you want: "ChatGPT, help me condense my market analysis into bullet points," or "Write a compelling narrative for my team introduction slide."

Before you can say "venture capital," you'll have eloquent, succinct, and engaging text that's just begging to be pasted onto beautiful slides.

Real-world Example

SUPPOSE YOUR STARTUP is a software-as-a-service (SaaS) platform for small pet groomers.

Bad Presentation: "We're selling software to pet groomers. The pet industry is big."

Good Presentation with ChatGPT: "Welcome to FurPal, the one-stop SaaS solution transforming small pet grooming businesses. With a $9 billion potential market and proprietary algorithms, we make appointment management, inventory tracking, and customer relations seamless. Already 50 groomers are reporting a 40% increase in operational efficiency using our beta version."

Notice the difference? The second version narrates a compelling story in the language investors understand: problem, solution, opportunity.

The Final Bow

AND THERE WE HAVE IT—YOUR complete guide to crafting investor presentations that not only inform but also inspire, thanks to the power of ChatGPT. Whether you're a seasoned entrepreneur or a startup neophyte, these AI-enabled techniques can elevate your presentation from a mere slide deck to a compelling narrative. Let's reinforce this knowledge with a few quick tips:

Tip 1: Less Is More

RESIST THE TEMPTATION to overstuff your slides. Use ChatGPT to help you condense information into digestible pieces, letting visuals and your own voice fill in the gaps.

Tip 2: Practice Makes Perfect

USE CHATGPT TO CREATE practice scripts or Q&A sessions that simulate what you'll face during the real presentation. The more prepared you are, the more confident you'll feel.

Tip 3: A/B Test Your Presentation

IF POSSIBLE, CREATE multiple versions of your slide deck and use ChatGPT to analyze feedback on each. This will help you hone in on the most effective elements to include.

AI isn't just a tool; it's your collaborative partner in crafting presentations that resonate. With ChatGPT's assistance, you're no longer aiming to just "get through" a presentation—you're striving to captivate, educate, and persuade. In essence, you're not just pitching your business, you're telling a compelling story that opens doors to new partnerships and opportunities.

Chapter 6: Polishing Your Investor Communications

Investor communications, the mingling cocktail party of the startup journey. At this soirée, the hors d'oeuvres are your monthly reports, the cocktails are your quarterly summaries, and the main course is your annual review. Now, if only there were a way to guarantee your missives are as smooth as a single malt whiskey and not as jarring as a tequila slammer.

The Art of the Schmooze

TALKING TO INVESTORS isn't like chatting with your college buddies. This is a sophisticated dance, where one wrong step could send you tumbling. Investors need reassurance, updates, and most of all, reasons to continue supporting you. All this calls for a style of communication that is both professional and engaging.

The Essentials of Investor Communique

REGULAR UPDATES ARE crucial—financial performance, milestones reached, challenges faced, and so on. These updates shouldn't just be dry facts; they should tell a story of your journey, punctuated by hard numbers and soft charms alike.

ChatGPT's Communication Clinic

IMAGINE IF YOU HAD a personal communications advisor who could draft or edit these critical messages for you. Well, buckle up, because ChatGPT is ready to step into that role! Whether you need to construct a delicate email announcing a setback or a triumphant report celebrating a major milestone, ChatGPT can help you craft it.

For instance, you could ask, "ChatGPT, can you help me draft a monthly investor update that highlights our new product launch?" or "Generate a quarterly summary that delicately addresses our lower-than-expected revenue."

Real-world Example

LET'S SAY YOUR STARTUP has had a challenging quarter with a major product delay.

Bad Communication: "Product's late. Had issues. Working on it."

Good Communication with ChatGPT: "While we aimed to launch our groundbreaking product this quarter, unforeseen challenges have delayed our timeline. Nevertheless, these hurdles have provided invaluable insights, making us even more committed to delivering a superior product. We appreciate your ongoing support and will keep you updated on our progress."

See how the second version maintains a positive spin without glossing over the facts? That's the art of investor communication.

Toasting to the Future

BY MAINTAINING POLISHED, ChatGPT-assisted communication with your investors, you're doing more than just ticking a box—you're building relationships. You're showing your backers that they didn't just invest in a business; they invested in a visionary leader who knows how to navigate both calm seas and stormy weather.

As we wrap up this invaluable chapter on perfecting your investor communications, it's essential to recognize that the power of ChatGPT goes beyond drafting emails or reports. It can be the extra pair of "digital eyes" that refines your messaging into clear, impactful language that stands out. Before we go, let's consider some useful tips to remember:

Tip 1: Consistency Is Key

WHETHER IT'S A SHAREHOLDER report, a newsletter, or an announcement, maintain consistent tone and language across all communications. ChatGPT can be trained to adhere to your specific brand voice, ensuring uniformity.

Tip 2: Double-Check for Sensitivity

USE CHATGPT TO FLAG any language that might be misunderstood or potentially problematic. The last thing you want is to create unwanted controversy with a poorly chosen word or phrase.

Tip 3: Automate Recurring Communications

IF YOU REGULARLY SEND out updates or financial reports, set up ChatGPT to automate these documents, tailoring only the updated figures and news. This saves you time for strategic thinking and decision-making.

The technology available to us is evolving, and so should our approach to investor communications. ChatGPT enables us to create well-polished, tailored messaging that not only informs but also engages investors on a deeper level. In this digital age, mastering the art of communication is no longer an option but a necessity.

So, as we conclude, think about this: How can you leverage ChatGPT to redefine the quality and impact of your investor communications?

Chapter 7: Utilizing ChatGPT for Networking and Relationship Building

———

Networking—the social dance that everyone knows they should be doing but few really enjoy. It's like being at a party where you don't know anyone, except here, the appetizers are LinkedIn connections and the main course is venture capital. While some entrepreneurs have the gift of the gab, others find networking as enjoyable as a root canal. Whichever camp you fall into, ChatGPT is here to make your life easier.

The Networking Nitty-Gritty

LOVE IT OR LOATHE IT(I really do loathe it), networking is essential. It's not just about getting your next round of funding, it's about advice, partnership opportunities, and building a reputation in your industry. Each email, message, or post you send out to your network is an opportunity to make a lasting impression.

The Digital Wingman

SURE, CHATGPT CAN'T attend cocktail events or hand out your business cards, but it can be your digital wingman. Want to reach out to an industry influencer? ChatGPT can help you craft an engaging message that's personalized but not creepy, formal but not robotic.

"ChatGPT, can you help me write a LinkedIn message to Jane Doe, a leader in renewable energy, to discuss potential collaboration?" With a prompt like that, ChatGPT will conjure a message that doesn't just end up as another unread notification for the recipient.

Real-world Example

LET'S SAY YOU'RE REACHING out to a high-profile angel investor.

Bad Message: "Hi, I've got a startup. Want to invest?"

Good Message with ChatGPT: "Hello [Investor's Name], I recently came across your insightful comments on AI in healthcare. As the founder of MedTech AI, a startup focused on streamlining patient care through artificial intelligence, I'd love to discuss the potential of a strategic partnership. Would you be open to a brief call next week?"

That second message not only shows you've done your homework but also outlines mutual benefits. It's the difference between a cold call and a warm introduction.

The Virtual Handshake

IF YOU'RE SKEPTICAL about using AI for such a personal aspect of business, consider this: How many opportunities have you missed because you couldn't find the right words, or simply didn't have the time? With ChatGPT by your side, you're not replacing the personal touch; you're enhancing it.

In the age of digital transformation, using ChatGPT as a tool for networking and relationship-building is no longer a novelty; it's a necessity. Your networking game can be revolutionized with a bit of AI intervention, opening doors you didn't even know existed. Before we move on, let's sum up with some actionable tips:

Tip 1: Segment Your Network

UTILIZE CHATGPT TO categorize your network into segments such as 'investors,' 'peers,' or 'mentors.' This allows for targeted and effective communication tailored to each group, making your outreach more impactful.

Tip 2: Set Up Reminders for Follow-ups

ONE OF THE MOST CRUCIAL aspects of networking is timely follow-up. Use ChatGPT to set up reminders and even draft follow-up messages to keep the conversation going after the initial meet.

Tip 3: Always Be Updating

YOUR NETWORK IS NOT a static entity; it's ever-evolving. Use ChatGPT to continually update your contact information, business achievements, and news, making it easier to share relevant updates with your network.

As we conclude this chapter, consider this: Networking is more than just a numbers game; it's about creating meaningful, lasting relationships. How will you use ChatGPT to turn every meet and greet into a potential stepping stone for future collaborations and investment opportunities? The journey of unlocking the potential of networking with ChatGPT starts with you, and what better time to start than now?

Chapter 9: Auto-generating Financial Forecasts

F inancial forecasts can be the bane of an entrepreneur's existence. Yet, they're vital in attracting investments. The challenge lies in their complexity and the need for meticulous accuracy. So, how can ChatGPT help you whip up some solid numbers that could charm even the most hard-nosed investor?

Understanding the Basics

FIRST OFF, CHATGPT can explain the foundational elements of a financial forecast, from revenue projections to cash flow statements. If you're lost, a simple prompt like "ChatGPT, can you explain the basics of financial forecasting?" will yield a concise tutorial.

Data Crunching and Assumptions

WHILE CHATGPT CAN'T run the numbers for you, it can help you brainstorm the variables and assumptions you should consider. A question like, "ChatGPT, what are common assumptions in financial forecasts for tech startups?" will provide you a comprehensive list tailored to your sector.

Real-world Example

LET'S SAY YOU'RE PREPARING for a crucial pitch meeting.

Without ChatGPT: You could be wrangling spreadsheets until the wee hours of the morning, doubting every number you put down.

With ChatGPT: You have a structured outline and list of considerations that can guide you as you fill in those intimidating Excel cells, reducing errors and stress.

Templates and Sample Text

CHATGPT CAN GENERATE textual explanations that accompany your numbers, which can be especially useful in presentations or investor meetings. Simply ask, "ChatGPT, can you help me write an explanation for our revenue projections?" and you'll receive a well-crafted passage that helps you communicate your data more effectively.

Financial forecasting can often feel like navigating through a maze in the dark. With ChatGPT by your side, you've got yourself a high-powered flashlight and a map. This technology simplifies the often arduous task of creating financial forecasts, turning it into a manageable, even enjoyable, part of your business planning.

Tip 1: Quality Over Quantity

WHILE IT MIGHT BE TEMPTING to produce as many forecasts as possible, focus on creating a few highly accurate and detailed projections. ChatGPT can help you review, tweak, and polish these forecasts, ensuring that they resonate with potential investors.

Tip 2: Periodic Updates

FINANCIAL FORECASTS are not a "set it and forget it" kind of task. Make it a practice to update them periodically. Use ChatGPT to compare actual results with predictions, helping you refine future forecasts.

Tip 3: Leverage Sensitivity Analysis

UTILIZE CHATGPT TO run multiple scenarios—best case, worst case, and most likely—to provide a well-rounded view of your financial future. This adds an extra layer of depth to your forecasts and makes them more robust.

To wrap up, it's crucial to remember that financial forecasts are more than just numbers on a spreadsheet; they are a testament to your startup's potential and your capability as an entrepreneur. So, arm yourself with ChatGPT, and make those numbers sing the sweet melody of success.

In the next chapter, we're diving into the endless sea of possibilities that is business idea brainstorming with ChatGPT. Buckle up; it's going to be an enlightening ride.

Chapter 9: Brainstorming Business Ideas

———

In the infancy of your startup journey, the most critical step is coming up with a business idea that's both innovative and viable. This is often a roadblock that many budding entrepreneurs face. Thankfully, with ChatGPT, brainstorming business ideas can be a walk in the park.

Ideation Techniques

CHATGPT CAN INTRODUCE you to a variety of ideation methods, like the SCAMPER technique (Substitute, Combine, Adapt, Modify, Put to another use, Eliminate, Reverse). Just ask, "ChatGPT, can you explain the SCAMPER technique for brainstorming?" and you'll get a quick rundown.

Target Market Insights

CHATGPT CAN ASSIST you in identifying gaps in the market that your startup could fill. A simple prompt like, "ChatGPT, what are some underserved markets in the technology sector?" can spark a list of opportunities for you to consider.

Real-world Example

IMAGINE YOU'RE SITTING at a coffee shop, frustrated with the lack of good ideas.

Without ChatGPT: You could be doodling on napkins, struggling to think outside the box.

With ChatGPT: You could shoot a quick prompt into your smartphone and get a list of ten intriguing business ideas tailored to your interests and skills.

Quick Validation

ONCE YOU HAVE A LIST of potential ideas, ChatGPT can help you craft questions or surveys for quick market validation. Just ask, "ChatGPT, what are some questions to validate a business idea?" and you'll have a list ready for your target audience.

Brainstorming may look like a chaotic process, a storm of thoughts swirling in your brain, but with ChatGPT, you can turn this storm into a finely tuned symphony of ideas. The AI can be a co-conductor, helping you shape, refine, and explore new avenues of thought that you might not have ventured down otherwise.

Tip 1: Use Prompt Variations

INSTEAD OF ASKING CHATGPT, "What's a good business idea?" try variations like, "What are some untapped markets in 2023?" or "Suggest some businesses that can be started with a small investment." The change in phrasing can yield diverse and more targeted results.

Tip 2: Layer Your Ideas

ONCE YOU HAVE A PRIMARY idea, don't stop there. Use ChatGPT to explore secondary or even tertiary business opportunities that can stem from that main concept. Think of it as an idea tree that keeps sprouting new branches.

Tip 3: Frequent Reality Checks

FOR EVERY PROMISING idea, ask ChatGPT to outline potential challenges or roadblocks. This can save you time and energy by helping you preemptively address or altogether avoid issues.

To sum up, the brainstorming process is a treasure trove of opportunities waiting to be discovered. With ChatGPT as your trusted first mate, you're not just blindly searching for treasure; you're navigating your ship with a map that marks the X right where it should be.

In the next chapter, we're tackling the art and science of crafting a compelling business plan. Trust us, with ChatGPT in your toolkit, it's going to be less 'Mission Impossible' and more 'Mission Probable

Chapter 10: Writing Business Plans

———

Writing a business plan is like constructing the foundation of a building. It needs to be strong, detailed, and comprehensive to support the towering structure of your startup dream. While you could try to pull it off on your own, why not seek a little help from your friendly neighborhood ChatGPT?

Structure Made Simple

A BUSINESS PLAN HAS various components—executive summary, market analysis, organization structure, and so on. If you're not sure how to organize these, ChatGPT can help. Just ask, "ChatGPT, what is the standard structure of a business plan?" and you'll receive a well-organized template.

Content Generation

FOR EACH SECTION OF your business plan, ChatGPT can help you draft content. If you're stuck on the market analysis section, for example, you could ask, "ChatGPT, can you help me write the market analysis section of my business plan?" And voila! You get a draft that you can refine and customize.

Real-world Example

SUPPOSE YOU HAVE A meeting with a potential investor in a week.

Without ChatGPT: You might be scrambling to get your business plan in order, foregoing sleep and sanity.

With ChatGPT: You have a structured, well-thought-out business plan that's been reviewed and revised multiple times, all ready to impress.

Financial Projections

CHATGPT CAN ALSO GUIDE you on how to articulate your financial projections within your business plan. Although it can't perform calculations, it can help you phrase your assumptions and projections convincingly.

Crafting a business plan is akin to laying down the foundation of a skyscraper. One wrong move and everything could come tumbling down. However, when you have ChatGPT on your side, it's like having a master architect reviewing every blueprint and making sure every brick is perfectly in place.

Tip 1: Modular Approach

INSTEAD OF WRITING a business plan from scratch, consider asking ChatGPT to draft individual sections like the Executive Summary, Market Analysis, or Financial Projections. This modular approach will give you a clearer perspective on each aspect of your business.

Tip 2: Cross-Referencing Data

ONCE YOU HAVE YOUR first draft, use ChatGPT to compare your business plan against market standards or case studies within your industry. This ensures your plan is not just comprehensive but also competitive.

Tip 3: Seek Alternative Scenarios

IT'S ALWAYS GOOD TO prepare for the best and the worst. Ask ChatGPT to generate a best-case, worst-case, and most-likely scenario for your business. This helps in foreseeing potential challenges and solutions.

In essence, ChatGPT serves as your digital co-founder when it comes to drafting a meticulous business plan. With the AI's insights, you're not just building castles in the sky; you're laying down solid foundations for empires of the future.

On the horizon of our next chapter, we have the mesmerizing art of creating catchy taglines and mission statements. With ChatGPT by your side, you're not just aiming for memorable; you're scripting unforgettable.

Chapter 11: Creating Catchy Taglines or Mission Statements

———

A memorable tagline or a compelling mission statement can serve as the soul of your startup. It can grab attention, inspire your team, and build trust with investors and customers alike. But crafting such a nugget of wisdom can be challenging. That's where ChatGPT comes in to lend a creative hand.

Elements of a Great Tagline

NOT SURE WHAT MAKES a tagline resonate? Ask ChatGPT, "What are the elements of a catchy tagline?" and it will break down the fundamentals for you, such as brevity, clarity, and emotional appeal.

Brainstorming Bonanza

YOU COULD SPEND HOURS thinking of a tagline, or you could consult ChatGPT for a brainstorming session. A simple prompt like, "ChatGPT, give me tagline ideas for a sustainable fashion brand," will yield an array of suggestions for you to consider.

Real-world Example

IMAGINE YOU'RE PREPPING for a trade show and need to finalize your marketing materials.

Without ChatGPT: You might get bogged down with multiple revisions and second-guessing yourself.

With ChatGPT: You'll have a set of fresh taglines and mission statements at your fingertips, ready to dazzle your audience.

Mission Statement Mastery

A MISSION STATEMENT is not just a few lines of text; it's your startup's north star. ChatGPT can assist you in crafting a mission statement that perfectly encapsulates your startup's essence. Just type, "ChatGPT, help me write a mission statement for a tech-for-good startup," and watch the magic happen.

Creating a tagline or mission statement isn't just about cobbling together a few words that sound good. It's about encapsulating your brand's ethos, vision, and unique value proposition in a line that sticks. With ChatGPT, you're not just brainstorming; you're strategizing to make every word count.

Tip 1: Test Multiple Versions

DON'T SETTLE FOR THE first catchy line that ChatGPT generates. Test a few versions to gauge how each resonates with your intended audience. Use these variations in consumer tests to identify which sticks.

Tip 2: Adapt for Different Platforms

YOUR TAGLINE OR MISSION statement may appear on various platforms, from social media to product packaging. Ask ChatGPT to adapt your chosen line for different character limits or formats. This ensures that your message stays potent, irrespective of where it's seen.

Tip 3: Keep Iterating

EVEN AFTER YOU'VE NAILED a tagline or mission statement, keep testing and refining it. Markets change, consumers evolve, and your brand grows. Use ChatGPT to periodically reassess and refine your tagline or mission statement to ensure it remains as relevant as your evolving brand.

Harnessing ChatGPT for your tagline or mission statement is like having a seasoned brand strategist in your corner, ensuring that your brand doesn't just fit into conversations but becomes the conversation.

As we turn the pages to our next chapter, we delve into the dynamic world of enhancing investor presentation decks. Gone are the days of mundane slides and bullet points; with ChatGPT, you're aiming to captivate and convince. Are you set to take your investor communications to a whole new level?

Chapter 12: Enhancing the Investor Presentation Deck

You've got one shot at impressing a room full of investors. Your pitch deck can either make you the toast of the evening or just another forgettable face in the crowd. ChatGPT can help you craft a presentation that investors won't easily forget.

Building the Deck

CREATING A PITCH DECK can be daunting, but ChatGPT can guide you through each slide, suggesting what to include and what to leave out. Type, "ChatGPT, what are the key slides in an investor pitch deck?" and you'll get a checklist that serves as a foundation for your presentation.

Tailored Content

CHATGPT CAN HELP YOU with specific slides, generating content that matches your startup's narrative. Ask, "ChatGPT, how should I present my business model in the pitch deck?" and you'll get a detailed outline or even complete paragraphs that you can plug into your slides.

Real-world Example

LET'S SAY YOU'RE PULLING an all-nighter before the big pitch.

Without ChatGPT: You could be staring at a screen, paralyzed by indecision and overwhelm.

With ChatGPT: You're briskly moving from slide to slide, with ChatGPT aiding in content creation, freeing you up to focus on practice and delivery.

Visual Storytelling

THOUGH CHATGPT CAN'T design slides, it can help you articulate what kind of visuals would support your content best. A quick prompt like, "ChatGPT, what kind of visuals should accompany my market analysis slide?" can offer valuable insights.

Creating an investor presentation deck is more than just a cut-and-paste job from your business plan. It's an art form that combines data, storytelling, and persuasion into a concise package. ChatGPT is your backstage artist, your prompter, and your strategist all rolled into one, ensuring that your slides not only inform but also impress.

Tip 1: Visual Consistency

YOUR PRESENTATION SHOULD be a visual treat, but it also needs a consistent aesthetic. Use ChatGPT to generate color schemes, font choices, or design motifs that can be used throughout your deck to maintain a cohesive look.

Tip 2: Story Arc

A GREAT PRESENTATION tells a story. Use ChatGPT to outline a compelling story arc for your presentation. Start with a challenge, introduce your solution, and end with your vision for the future. Make your investors the heroes who can make that future possible.

Tip 3: Backup Slides

ALWAYS HAVE A SET OF backup slides prepared for the Q&A session. Use ChatGPT to anticipate possible questions and generate slides with additional data, case studies, or testimonials that can add weight to your answers.

With ChatGPT at your disposal, your investor presentation deck becomes a dynamic tool that's not just aimed at showcasing your business, but at transforming your audience into stakeholders.

So, as we flip over to the next chapter, we're going to explore the utility of AI in conducting a thorough SWOT Analysis.

Chapter 13: AI-assisted SWOT Analysis

———

A SWOT (Strengths, Weaknesses, Opportunities, Threats) analysis is more than just a fancy acronym—it's an insightful exercise that can offer a panoramic view of your startup's landscape. While the human mind is fallible and biased, the logic-driven assistance from ChatGPT can bring objectivity and thoroughness to this crucial task.

Breaking Down SWOT

ARE YOU UNSURE WHAT goes under each category of a SWOT analysis? Just ask ChatGPT, "What are typical elements of a SWOT analysis?" and you'll get a comprehensive list of what could go under Strengths, Weaknesses, Opportunities, and Threats.

Data-Driven Insights

YOU CAN FEED MARKET data, customer feedback, or even snippets of competitor reviews into ChatGPT. It can help you incorporate these data points into a SWOT analysis, providing more substance to your insights.

Real-world Example

SUPPOSE YOU'RE IN A strategy meeting with your team.

Without ChatGPT: The SWOT analysis might be prone to groupthink, or worse, become a superficial exercise with no actionable insights.

With ChatGPT: You can present a detailed, impartial SWOT analysis that opens the floor to deeper, more productive discussions.

Decision-making Aid

YOUR SWOT ANALYSIS isn't just an investor-pleasing exercise; it's a vital tool for decision-making. ChatGPT can help here by prompting questions based on your SWOT. Type, "ChatGPT, what strategies can we formulate based on these strengths?" and see your business strategies take a more informed shape.

The terrain of business strategy is filled with pitfalls and opportunities. Knowing how to navigate through it with agility can be your ticket to success. And a SWOT analysis, when done correctly, is like your compass, guiding you through the murkiness of business challenges. Thanks to AI-assisted capabilities, such as those offered by ChatGPT, you can supercharge your SWOT analysis to ensure you're not just ticking boxes but making strategic moves.

Tip 1: Dynamic SWOT

A SWOT ANALYSIS ISN'T a one-time affair. With ChatGPT, you can keep your SWOT dynamically updated. Use real-time data and market trends to frequently update your strengths, weaknesses, opportunities, and threats.

Tip 2: Cross-Referencing

TO MAKE THE MOST OF your SWOT analysis, cross-reference the elements. For instance, look at how your strengths can capitalize on current opportunities or how to use your strengths to counteract threats. ChatGPT can help you generate scenarios or action plans based on these cross-references.

Tip 3: Prioritization

NOT ALL ELEMENTS IN a SWOT analysis are created equal. Use ChatGPT to help prioritize issues or opportunities based on parameters such as feasibility, impact, and urgency. This will guide you to focus your energy and resources where they will be most effective.

Remember, technology isn't just about automating tasks; it's about augmenting our capabilities and helping us make better decisions. And with that, we will venture into the art and science of drafting and refining investment contracts in our next chapter.

Chapter 14: Drafting and Refining Investment Contracts

———

Securing investment is a thrilling milestone, but what follows is often far less glamorous: wading through the murky waters of investment contracts. Luckily, ChatGPT can act as your buoy, guiding you through the legalese and helping you draft documents that protect your interests.

Clauses and Conditions

BEFORE YOU GET LOST in a labyrinth of legal jargon, ask ChatGPT, "What are the key clauses in an investment contract?" You'll get a straightforward list that you can discuss with your legal advisor, ensuring you don't miss any crucial elements.

Templates to Start With

WHILE IT'S ADVISABLE to consult a legal expert for finalizing contracts, ChatGPT can help you get started by generating a basic template. A prompt like, "ChatGPT, show me a sample investment contract for a tech startup," will provide a solid starting point.

Real-world Example

IMAGINE YOU'RE IN INITIAL discussions with potential investors.

Without ChatGPT: You might delay negotiations because you're unsure about the contract specifics, or worse, agree to unfavorable terms out of ignorance.

With ChatGPT: You're equipped with a preliminary contract draft and a list of key clauses, helping you negotiate from a position of strength.

Fine-tuning the Language

SOMETIMES LEGAL LANGUAGE can be unnecessarily complex, leading to misunderstandings. ChatGPT can assist you in simplifying and clarifying the language. Just type, "ChatGPT, can you simplify this clause for me?" and you'll get a more digestible version.

In the intricate ballet of entrepreneurship, legal agreements often serve as the stage on which your business dances. They might not be the star of the show, but they certainly set the parameters for how freely and creatively you can move. By leveraging the capabilities of ChatGPT in drafting and refining your investment contracts, you're not just speeding up a tedious process; you're injecting a level of precision and customization often reserved for top-tier legal departments.

Tip 1: Clause Libraries

CONSIDER CREATING A library of standard clauses and terms that can be readily inserted into any investment contract. ChatGPT can help you assemble, categorize, and even suggest where these standard clauses could be most effectively used.

Tip 2: Version Control

KEEPING TRACK OF REVISIONS can be a nightmare when dealing with multiple stakeholders. Use ChatGPT to annotate changes, suggest edits, and keep an updated repository of versions. This way, you're never at risk of overlooking important modifications.

Tip 3: Compliance Checks

LEGAL LANDSCAPES ARE constantly changing. Use ChatGPT to help you stay abreast of relevant regulations and ensure that your contracts are compliant. Automated updates can flag any clauses that might be outdated or risky in light of new legislation.

As we close this chapter, we turn our focus to the dynamic realm of investor relations. How do you maintain an open line of communication that is as efficient as it is engaging? Well, brace yourself because our next chapter delves deep into automating investor relations communications. Trust me, this is a game-changer!

Chapter 15: Automating Investor Relations Communications

———

In the fast-paced world of startups, investor relations can often be relegated to a hurried email here and a quick update there. But maintaining consistent, professional communication with your investors is crucial. This is where ChatGPT can make a world of difference.

I really believe in getting this right. Not just as someone looking for investment but those you ask. I cannot remember how many times I have had people looking for investment and not remembering previous conversations or sending me some BS twelve months ago.

Regular Updates

CONSISTENCY IS KEY when it comes to investor relations. ChatGPT can assist you in drafting monthly or quarterly reports that keep your investors in the loop. Just type, "ChatGPT, help me draft a quarterly investor update," and you'll get a well-structured template.

Handling Queries

INVESTORS OFTEN HAVE questions that require prompt and thoughtful responses. ChatGPT can help you formulate replies that are not just timely but also comprehensive. Ask, "ChatGPT, how do I respond to an investor asking about our recent decline in monthly active users?" and you'll get a nuanced answer.

Real-world Example

LET'S CONSIDER YOU'RE swamped with work right before a major product launch.

Without ChatGPT: Investor communications might take a backseat, causing unnecessary stress and potentially damaging important relationships.

With ChatGPT: You can quickly generate updates or responses to investor queries, maintaining goodwill without sacrificing your focus on the product.

Automating Routine Interactions

USING SIMPLE CHATBOT frameworks, you can even integrate ChatGPT to handle routine investor queries in an automated but personalized manner. This allows you to manage your time more efficiently while ensuring that your investors feel attended to.

In the 24/7, always-on world of modern business, your investors are both your greatest advocates and your most attentive critics. Keeping them informed, engaged, and assured is not just a courtesy; it's a necessity. Employing ChatGPT in your investor relations strategy can be like hiring a full-time, exceptionally competent assistant whose sole task is to make your life simpler and your investors happier. That said, you're only as good as the tools you use and how you use them.

Tip 1: Timely Updates

USE CHATGPT TO SET reminders for sending out periodic updates to your investors, whether weekly, monthly, or quarterly.

Tip 2: Personalization

CUSTOMIZE EACH COMMUNICATION for specific investor groups. ChatGPT can help you tailor messages based on the investor's history, interests, and portfolio.

Tip 3: Automated Q&A

TRAIN CHATGPT TO ANSWER common questions that investors might ask, thus saving time on back-and-forths.

Tip 4: Real-Time Data Sharing

UTILIZE CHATGPT TO summarize and share real-time data like market trends, stock performance, or any other KPIs relevant to investors.

Tip 5: Crisis Communication

PREPARE PRE-SCRIPTED messages for various crisis scenarios. ChatGPT can help you draft these and deploy them at the right time.

Tip 6: Meeting Schedulers

USE CHATGPT TO SCHEDULE, reschedule, and remind both parties of upcoming meetings, webinars, or conference calls.

Tip 7: Feedback Loop

IMPLEMENT A SYSTEM where ChatGPT collects feedback from investors and analyzes it for patterns, providing you with actionable insights.

Tip 8: Media Monitoring

HAVE CHATGPT SCAN MEDIA channels for news related to your business or industry and summarize it for your investors.

Tip 9: Regulatory Compliance

LET CHATGPT HELP YOU keep track of regulations that impact investor relations and communications, ensuring you remain in compliance.

Tip 10: Sentiment Analysis

USE CHATGPT TO PERFORM sentiment analysis on investor communications, enabling you to adapt your strategy based on the mood and concerns of your investor base.

With those tips in your arsenal, you're well on your way to mastering the art of investor relations, one automated email at a time.

Chapter 16: Customizing Investor Outreach

When it comes to securing investment, one-size-fits-all just doesn't cut it. Investors are as diverse as the portfolios they manage, and so your outreach to them should be equally varied. ChatGPT offers a means to tailor your communications to fit the profile of each potential investor.

Identifying Investor Types

THE FIRST STEP IN CUSTOMIZATION is knowing your audience. ChatGPT can help you draft questions or surveys that you can send to potential investors to identify their interests. A prompt like, "ChatGPT, help me draft a survey for potential investors," can get you started.

Creating Targeted Pitches

BASED ON THE INFORMATION gathered, ChatGPT can assist you in creating investor pitches tailored to individual preferences. For example, some investors may prioritize sustainability, while others may focus on immediate ROI. ChatGPT can help you tweak your pitch to appeal to these specific preferences.

Real-world Example

SUPPOSE YOU'RE GETTING ready to pitch to an angel investor and a venture capital firm.

Without ChatGPT: You might end up using the same pitch for both, missing an opportunity to speak to their unique interests.

With ChatGPT: You could create two different versions of your pitch, each emphasizing the elements that are most likely to resonate with the respective investor types.

Automated Follow-ups

WE ALL KNOW THE IMPORTANCE of follow-up emails but often neglect them due to time constraints. ChatGPT can assist you in crafting follow-up emails that not only thank the investors for their time but also subtly remind them why your startup is worth investing in.

Reaching out to investors is far from a one-size-fits-all endeavor. Investors are as diverse as the projects they choose to back, and their motivations for investing can be just as varied. If you want to get through to them effectively, your outreach efforts need to be tailored to the individual. The potential for ChatGPT in this arena is transformative. With the right configuration and input, this technology can help you customize your outreach at scale, creating personalized experiences that can yield far better results than a mass-produced approach.

Tip 1: Segmentation

INVESTORS USUALLY FALL into different categories based on their interests, risk appetite, and investment size. ChatGPT can help you segment your investor list and customize messages accordingly.

Tip 2: Contextual Relevance

BEFORE REACHING OUT, make sure you gather as much context as possible about the investor. Use ChatGPT to keep a database that records their past behaviors, interactions, and preferences, and refer to this information to make your outreach more relevant.

Tip 3: Timely Follow-ups

USE CHATGPT TO AUTOMATE follow-up messages based on investor engagement. If an investor opens an email but doesn't reply, you could have a follow-up message automatically sent after a specific period.

Tip 4: A/B Testing

USE CHATGPT TO HELP design A/B tests for your outreach emails. This can help you understand what type of messaging resonates most with your target investors, allowing you to continuously refine your approach.

Tip 5: Personalized Recommendations

CHATGPT CAN GENERATE investment options based on the investor's profile. Offering these personalized recommendations can show the investor that you've done your homework, making them more likely to engage with you.

The importance of customizing your investor outreach cannot be overstated. By making your communications more relevant, timely, and personal, you're not just another startup looking for funds—you become a thoughtful entrepreneur who respects the investor's time and priorities.

Chapter 17: Virtual Role-play for Investor Negotiations

Negotiating with investors is often the high-stakes climax of months (or years) of hard work. Preparation is key, but mock negotiations with friends or team members can be awkward and unproductive. This is where ChatGPT can be a game-changer. Its one of those things that when you are starting out with your startup, most entrepreneurs get wrong, really wrong in some circumstances.

Role-play Scenarios

CHATGPT CAN SIMULATE various investor personas, from the skeptical hardliner to the overly enthusiastic novice. By interacting with these personas, you can practice your pitch, answer tough questions, and gauge investor reactions, all in a no-risk environment.

Real-time Feedback

ONE OF THE ADVANTAGES of using ChatGPT for role-playing is instant feedback. After each mock negotiation session, you can ask ChatGPT for a critique. Phrases like, "ChatGPT, how did I handle the question on our valuation?" can help you understand where you shine and where you need improvement.

Real-world Example

IMAGINE YOU HAVE A crucial meeting with a renowned venture capitalist next week.

Without ChatGPT: You may practice with colleagues, but the feedback may be sugarcoated or unhelpful.

With ChatGPT: You can conduct multiple rounds of rigorous, no-holds-barred practice sessions, fine-tuning your approach each time based on detailed feedback.

Overcoming Negotiation Jitters

MANY ENTREPRENEURS find negotiations stressful, which can lead to less-than-optimal outcomes. Virtual role-playing with ChatGPT can help lessen anxiety by familiarizing you with common questions, objections, and even curveballs that investors might throw your way.

The world of investor negotiations is fraught with variables, unknowns, and, quite often, surprises. Virtual role-playing for investor negotiations can be a powerful tool to practice your pitch, address objections, and fine-tune your delivery, all within a risk-free environment. With ChatGPT, you have a customizable platform that allows you to simulate a myriad of scenarios, from the most welcoming to the most challenging, to prepare you for the real deal.

Tip 1: Emulate Real Scenarios

USE CHATGPT TO EMULATE as many real-world scenarios as possible. From investors who are extremely cautious to those who are overly aggressive, practicing with a wide range of simulated characters can help you be better prepared for actual meetings.

Tip 2: Leverage Multi-Media

WHILE CHATGPT IS MAINLY text-based, it can be integrated into a broader multi-media role-play setup. Incorporate slides, data, or even video in your practice scenarios to make them more realistic.

Tip 3: Instant Feedback

CHATGPT CAN BE PROGRAMMED to provide instant feedback based on your responses. This allows you to correct mistakes or refine your tactics on the fly, enabling a quicker learning curve.

Tip 4: Recruit Team Involvement

USE CHATGPT TO CREATE role-playing scenarios for your entire team. Investor negotiations are often a team effort, and everyone should be prepared and aligned with the company's objectives and talking points.

Tip 5: Record and Review

IF POSSIBLE, RECORD your practice sessions. The logs generated by ChatGPT can be reviewed to analyze your performance. This also allows you to share the exercise with mentors or advisors who can provide additional feedback.

When it comes to investor negotiations, nothing replaces real-world experience. However, practicing with virtual role-play can certainly equip you with better tools and greater confidence to tackle the unpredictable road ahead.

Chapter 18: Curating Industry Trends and Statistics

Investors love data. It's the language they speak, and they expect you to be fluent. However, gathering relevant industry trends and statistics can be a time-consuming task. ChatGPT can serve as your data curator, helping you compile the necessary information to make your pitch more compelling.

The Importance of Data

SOLID DATA NOT ONLY substantiates your claims but also demonstrates your depth of knowledge about the industry. When you're aware of market trends, consumer behavior, and competitor landscapes, you present yourself as an entrepreneur who has done their homework.

How ChatGPT Can Help

WHILE CHATGPT CAN'T perform real-time data gathering from external databases, it can help you draft questions and templates for surveys, compile existing information into a coherent format, and help you put together a list of statistics to gather.

Real-world Example

LET'S SAY YOU'RE IN the renewable energy sector, seeking investment for a solar farm project.

Without ChatGPT: You might spend countless hours scouring reports, articles, and research papers to compile relevant data.

With ChatGPT: You can ask, "Help me create a list of important data points and statistics for a solar farm investment pitch." The model can guide you on what kind of data will be most appealing to investors and help you format it effectively.

Preparing a Data-Driven Pitch

ONCE YOU'VE GATHERED all the data, ChatGPT can assist in incorporating it into your pitch. From creating data visualization descriptions to framing statistics in a way that aligns with your narrative, ChatGPT is your statistical wordsmith.

The world of investor negotiations is fraught with variables, unknowns, and, quite often, surprises. Virtual role-playing for investor negotiations can be a powerful tool to practice your pitch, address objections, and fine-tune your delivery, all within a risk-free environment. With ChatGPT, you have a customizable platform that allows you to simulate a myriad of scenarios, from the most welcoming to the most challenging, to prepare you for the real deal.

Tip 1: Emulate Real Scenarios

USE CHATGPT TO EMULATE as many real-world scenarios as possible. From investors who are extremely cautious to those who are overly aggressive, practicing with a wide range of simulated characters can help you be better prepared for actual meetings.

Tip 2: Leverage Multi-Media

WHILE CHATGPT IS MAINLY text-based, it can be integrated into a broader multi-media role-play setup. Incorporate slides, data, or even video in your practice scenarios to make them more realistic.

Tip 3: Instant Feedback

CHATGPT CAN BE PROGRAMMED to provide instant feedback based on your responses. This allows you to correct mistakes or refine your tactics on the fly, enabling a quicker learning curve.

Tip 4: Recruit Team Involvement

USE CHATGPT TO CREATE role-playing scenarios for your entire team. Investor negotiations are often a team effort, and everyone should be prepared and aligned with the company's objectives and talking points.

Tip 5: Record and Review

IF POSSIBLE, RECORD your practice sessions. The logs generated by ChatGPT can be reviewed to analyze your performance. This also allows you to share the exercise with mentors or advisors who can provide additional feedback.

When it comes to investor negotiations, nothing replaces real-world experience. However, practicing with virtual role-play can certainly equip you with better tools and greater confidence to tackle the unpredictable road ahead.

Chapter 19: Setting up Virtual Investor Meet-and-Greets

―――

In the digital age, it's possible to meet potential investors without ever leaving your home. However, setting up virtual investor meet-and-greets involves more than just sending a Zoom invite. This chapter explores how ChatGPT can assist in organizing, preparing, and even following up on these important encounters.

The Preparation Phase

BEFORE THE MEETING, you'll need to gather investor profiles, set an agenda, and prepare talking points. Here's where ChatGPT can help:

- Investor Profiles: You can ask ChatGPT to draft questions to gather insights into the investor's background, investment philosophy, and interests.

- Agenda: A well-crafted agenda sets the tone for a productive meeting. ChatGPT can assist in generating an agenda that covers all essential points without overwhelming the attendees.

Real-world Example

SUPPOSE YOU HAVE THREE back-to-back virtual meetings with investors who have different interests and focus areas.

Without ChatGPT: You'd probably need a team to manage agendas, customize investor profiles, and come up with talking points.

With ChatGPT: Simply input the meeting details, and ChatGPT can generate personalized agendas, talking points, and even suggested questions for each meeting.

During the Meeting

WHILE CHATGPT CAN'T attend the meeting in your place, it can assist in real-time if you have a second device available. Think of it as a virtual cheat sheet that can help you with facts, statistics, or even to generate responses to unforeseen questions on the spot.

The Follow-Up

INVESTOR MEETINGS ARE as much about the follow-up as they are about the first impression. ChatGPT can assist in generating thank-you emails, summarizing meeting points, and even setting reminders to follow up on action items.

The journey to securing investment is a process that requires not just a compelling business case but also meaningful relationships. Virtual meet-and-greets provide an avenue to make these vital connections in a world where face-to-face interactions have limitations. Utilizing ChatGPT for these virtual sessions can streamline the process, add a touch of personalization, and perhaps most importantly, let you focus on what really matters: building genuine relationships with potential investors.

Tip 1: Test Your Tech

BEFORE CONDUCTING A virtual meet-and-greet, ensure that all the technical elements, including your ChatGPT setup, are functioning perfectly. Run a dry test to minimize any tech-related disruptions.

Tip 2: Personalization is Key

USE CHATGPT TO SEND personalized invitations or follow-up notes to investors based on their specific interests or past interactions. This adds a personal touch and makes your potential investors feel valued.

Tip 3: Prepopulate Topics

PRIORITIZE WHAT TOPICS or issues are most likely to be discussed and prep ChatGPT to handle those. This helps in guiding the conversation and ensuring you hit all the key points.

Tip 4: Multilingual Support

IF YOUR INVESTOR POOL is global, make sure that ChatGPT is ready to assist in multiple languages. This can be a game-changer in building rapport with international investors.

Tip 5: Real-Time Monitoring

MONITOR THE VIRTUAL meet-and-greet in real-time and use ChatGPT to provide immediate responses or data, as required. The quicker and more accurately you can answer investor queries, the better your chances at forming a lasting impression.

Chapter 20: Writing Press Releases for Funding Announcements

———

You've successfully secured investment. Hooray! But don't pop the champagne just yet; there's more work to be done. Announcing your funding to the world is a critical part of the investment cycle, and doing it right can create significant momentum for your venture. In this chapter, we'll explore how ChatGPT can assist you in crafting the perfect press release to announce your funding.

Why Press Releases Matter

A WELL-WRITTEN PRESS release can achieve multiple objectives:

- Visibility: It can attract attention from other potential investors, customers, and even future employees.

- Credibility: It adds a layer of legitimacy to your business, showing that it has garnered financial support from external parties.

- Momentum: It can create a 'buzz' around your brand, encouraging more interactions and engagement.

How ChatGPT Can Help

CHATGPT CAN ASSIST in various ways, from drafting the initial outline to finalizing the entire press release.

Headline Creation: The headline should be catchy yet informative. ChatGPT can generate several options for you to choose from.

Body Content: The model can help you structure the content in a way that's compelling and to the point, without missing any essential information.

Quotes: Every good press release includes quotes from the leadership team, and sometimes from investors. ChatGPT can help you draft these, making them sound natural and impactful.

Real-world Example

LET'S SAY YOU'VE RAISED funding for your health tech startup.

Without ChatGPT: You'd probably consult multiple templates online, hire a copywriter, or struggle to write one yourself.

With ChatGPT: You could simply ask, "Help me draft a press release for a health tech startup that just secured Series A funding." And voilà, you'd have a draft to work from in minutes.

Announcing a funding round is more than a celebratory moment—it's a strategic opportunity to reinforce your brand's story and capture the attention of a wider audience, including potential investors and customers. In this world of information overload, crafting a compelling press release can make or break your message. Leveraging ChatGPT can streamline this critical task, ensuring that your announcement is not only informative but also engaging and reflective of your brand's unique voice.

Tip 1: Keep it Newsworthy

ENSURE YOUR PRESS RELEASE contains elements that make it newsworthy. ChatGPT can assist by highlighting key information that should be in the spotlight.

Tip 2: A Strong Lead

YOUR FIRST PARAGRAPH should capture attention. Use ChatGPT to craft a lead that sums up the most critical aspects of your announcement.

Tip 3: Add Quotes

INCLUDE QUOTES FROM key stakeholders. ChatGPT can auto-generate these, which you can then modify to better match your authentic voice.

Tip 4: SEO Matters

CHATGPT CAN HELP IDENTIFY relevant keywords to include in your press release, increasing the likelihood it will be found and read.

Tip 5: Customization

USE CHATGPT TO CUSTOMIZE press releases for different media channels. A release for a tech blog may need different language than one aimed at a financial news outlet.

Tip 6: Imagery

DON'T FORGET TO ATTACH relevant images or infographics. ChatGPT can suggest what types of visuals might best support your narrative.

Tip 7: Conciseness

A PRESS RELEASE SHOULD be concise but comprehensive. Use ChatGPT to trim down your content to keep it focused and on-point.

Tip 8: Call to Action

INCLUDE A COMPELLING call to action. ChatGPT can generate options that align with your strategic goals, whether that's driving people to your website or encouraging shares on social media.

Tip 9: Review and Revise

BEFORE PUBLISHING, use ChatGPT to scan your press release for any grammatical errors or awkward phrasings. Quality assurance is key.

Tip 10: Monitoring Success

AFTER THE PRESS RELEASE is out, ChatGPT can assist in tracking its reach, engagement, and impact, allowing you to measure its effectiveness.

Chapter 21: Networking Email Templates

In the modern business landscape, networking is an indispensable tool. It can open doors, provide invaluable insights, and yes, connect you to potential investors. This chapter delves into how ChatGPT can supercharge your networking game by helping you craft impeccable email templates.

The Significance of Networking Emails

SENDING A WELL-THOUGHT-out email can make a lasting impression. However, it's not just about what you say but also how you say it. A well-crafted email can:

- Engage: An attention-grabbing subject line can make all the difference.

- Inform: Your email should convey the essential information without overwhelming the reader.

- Call to Action: Every email should have a purpose, guiding the reader on what to do next.

The Role of ChatGPT

CHATGPT CAN ASSIST you in each stage of your email drafting process:

Subject Line: Crafting the perfect subject line is an art. ChatGPT can provide several options tailored to your specific need.

Body Content: ChatGPT can help you structure the body of the email, ensuring it's concise yet informative.

Signature: Yes, even your email signature can be optimized. ChatGPT can help you create one that provides all necessary contact information in a neat and attractive layout.

Real-world Example

SUPPOSE YOU WANT TO reach out to an investor who has shown interest in renewable energy projects.

Without ChatGPT: You'd likely spend hours mulling over every word, concerned about tone and content.

With ChatGPT: Simply ask, "Help me draft a networking email for an investor interested in renewable energy." ChatGPT will provide a comprehensive template that you can personalize further, saving you time and mental energy.

In the digital age, networking goes far beyond face-to-face interactions; it often starts with an email. Crafting a networking email that stands out and effectively communicates your objectives is vital. Your words need to resonate, making the recipient feel both special and engaged. This chapter has shown you how ChatGPT can automate the process of generating networking emails, tailoring each message to align with your business goals and the person you're trying to connect with.

Tip 1: Personalization is Key

USING CHATGPT, YOU can personalize emails beyond just the recipient's name. Think industry jargon, shared interests, or mutual connections to make the email more relatable.

Tip 2: Clear and Direct Subject Lines

CHATGPT CAN HELP YOU create subject lines that are both intriguing and straightforward, increasing the likelihood of your email being opened.

Tip 3: Structure and Flow

GOOD NETWORKING EMAILS have a logical structure: an introduction, the main message, and a call-to-action. ChatGPT can help structure your email to guide the reader smoothly from one point to the next.

Tip 4: Follow-Up Mechanism

CHATGPT CAN AUTOMATE follow-up emails based on triggers like no response within a certain time frame, ensuring you remain on the radar but not annoying.

Tip 5: Proofreading

BEFORE HITTING SEND, leverage ChatGPT to double-check your email for any grammar or spelling errors. First impressions count, and a well-proofed email sets the right tone.

Armed with these tips and ChatGPT's capabilities, you're now well-equipped to scale your networking efforts without losing the personal touch that makes meaningful professional relationships possible.

Chapter 22: Due Diligence Document Preparation

———

Most investment deals fail due to DD. If your investor thinks there is a can of spaghetti to get through then it will make them burn calories and switch off.

The phrase "due diligence" may sound as exciting as watching paint dry, but it's a make-or-break step in the investment process. As the startup founder, you have to provide documents that prove your business is a worthwhile investment. In this chapter, we'll discuss how ChatGPT can help ease the process of preparing these crucial documents.

Why Due Diligence Documents Are Essential

THESE DOCUMENTS SERVE as the bedrock for the investor's decision-making process. They contain all the essential information about your business, including but not limited to:

- Financial records

- Business plans

- Market research

- Legal compliance documents

How ChatGPT Can Assist

WHILE CHATGPT CAN'T replace a financial advisor or a legal expert, it can help streamline the preparation process:

Document List: ChatGPT can generate a checklist of all the documents you'll likely need for due diligence.

Template Generation: For non-sensitive, text-based documents like business plans or market research reports, ChatGPT can help draft templates that you can fill in.

Guidance: If you're unsure about what to include in a particular section of a document, ChatGPT can offer suggestions based on industry standards.

Real-world Example

LET'S SAY YOU'RE ABOUT to go through due diligence for your edtech startup.

Without ChatGPT: You'd spend hours, if not days, doing research to ensure you've got all the right documents and that they're up to snuff.

With ChatGPT: You could ask, "What documents do I need for due diligence for an edtech startup?" and get a detailed list almost instantly. You could then ask for assistance in preparing individual documents, saving you a great deal of time and stress.

Due diligence is a critical phase in any investment process. Whether you're on the giving or receiving end of the scrutiny, being prepared can make or break the deal. With ChatGPT, you can automate the creation of key due diligence documents, ensuring accuracy, comprehensiveness, and timeliness. Through the power of automated text generation, you can focus more on strategy and relationship-building, confident that the document preparation is in good hands.

Tip 1: Start Early

DON'T WAIT FOR THE due diligence phase to get all your documents in order. ChatGPT can help you create a due diligence checklist well in advance.

Tip 2: Be Comprehensive

FROM FINANCIALS TO legal papers, ChatGPT can ensure you're not missing any vital information. Double-check your list for any sector-specific documentation you might need.

Tip 3: Prioritize Transparency

CHATGPT CAN HELP YOU draft clear and detailed explanations for any red flags in your business history, making sure you're as transparent as possible with prospective investors.

Tip 4: Utilize Templates

USE CHATGPT TO GENERATE templates for different types of due diligence documents, tailored to different industries or stages of investment.

Tip 5: Version Control

CHATGPT CAN ASSIST you in tracking document versions, making sure everyone involved has the most updated information.

Tip 6: Metadata Matters

ENHANCE YOUR DOCUMENTS with metadata like timestamps and author names, which ChatGPT can automatically include for you.

Tip 7: Automated Summaries

FOR LENGTHY DOCUMENTS, use ChatGPT to generate executive summaries highlighting the most critical points for quick reference.

Tip 8: Legal Language

USE CHATGPT'S LANGUAGE models trained in legalese to help draft contractual clauses, disclaimers, and other legal documents.

Tip 9: Confidentiality Measures

CHATGPT CAN GENERATE non-disclosure agreements and other confidentiality documents to protect sensitive information during the due diligence process.

Tip 10: Post-Due Diligence Follow-up

AFTER THE DUE DILIGENCE is complete, use ChatGPT to send personalized follow-up emails to stakeholders, summarizing the outcomes and next steps.

By mastering these tips and leveraging the power of ChatGPT, you're setting yourself up for a smoother, more efficient due diligence process.

Chapter 23: Scripting Video Pitches

As video content becomes an ever-increasing part of our digital diet, a well-executed video pitch can be an incredibly powerful tool for winning over investors. In this chapter, we'll explore how ChatGPT can assist in scripting a compelling video pitch that leaves a lasting impression.

The Power of a Video Pitch

A VIDEO PITCH CAN HUMANIZE your startup, showcase your product in action, and create an emotional connection with potential investors. The elements of a successful video pitch usually include:

- A compelling introduction

- The problem statement

- Your solution

- Business model

- Call to action

How ChatGPT Can Help

CHATGPT CAN BE A VALUABLE asset in crafting a script that strikes the right balance between information and engagement:

Script Outline: ChatGPT can help you generate an outline, ensuring that all key points are covered.

Engaging Narratives: ChatGPT can assist in creating a storytelling approach to make the pitch more relatable.

Tone Matching: Whether you're aiming for a formal tone or something more conversational, ChatGPT can adapt the script accordingly.

Real-world Example

IMAGINE YOU'RE IN THE healthcare technology sector and need a video pitch.

Without ChatGPT: You might spend days writing, rewriting, and fine-tuning every sentence, still unsure if the script will resonate with investors.

With ChatGPT: You could simply input, "Create a video pitch script for a healthcare technology startup." Within minutes, you'd have a well-structured, engaging script ready for review and personalization.

In today's digital age, a video pitch can be a powerful tool to capture investors' attention. When scripted well, it can convey your business concept, personality, and enthusiasm far better than a written proposal could. ChatGPT can be your collaborative partner in scripting video pitches that are not only compelling but also concise, clear, and investor-ready. Whether you're a startup founder or an established business looking for investment, making use of AI to polish your video pitch can provide that extra edge you need to stand out in a competitive market.

Tip 1: Clear Structure

USE CHATGPT TO OUTLINE a clear structure for your pitch, dividing it into sections like introduction, problem statement, solution, and call-to-action.

Tip 2: Focus on the Hook

ENGAGE YOUR AUDIENCE within the first few seconds. ChatGPT can help you brainstorm hooks that are both interesting and relevant to your business model.

Tip 3: Cut the Jargon

UNLESS IT'S INDUSTRY-specific and necessary, avoid using jargon. ChatGPT can help you simplify complex concepts into layman's terms.

Tip 4: Personalize the Message

USE CHATGPT TO INSERT tailored messages or anecdotes that can resonate with specific investors you're targeting.

Tip 5: Get to the Point

CHATGPT CAN HELP YOU edit your script to keep it short and impactful, focusing only on the most critical elements of your pitch.

Tip 6: Leverage Visuals

CHATGPT CAN GENERATE descriptions for visuals, infographics, or slide decks that can supplement your video pitch effectively.

Tip 7: Add a Human Element

IF THERE ARE TESTIMONIALS or endorsements, use ChatGPT to script those sections in a way that adds credibility and a human element to your pitch.

Tip 8: Script the Conclusion Carefully

CHATGPT CAN HELP YOU summarize the key points and end with a persuasive call-to-action that leaves a lasting impression.

Tip 9: Rehearse, Revise, Rehearse

USE CHATGPT'S TEXT-to-speech functionalities to hear your script and make adjustments as needed before the final take.

Tip 10: Seek Feedback

ONCE YOUR SCRIPT IS ready, use ChatGPT to generate questions that you can use to seek constructive feedback from peers or mentors.

By utilizing these tips and leveraging the capabilities of ChatGPT, your video pitch is sure to be more persuasive, professional, and effective

Chapter 24: Real-time Translation for International Investors

---

We live in a globalized world, where investments can cross borders as easily as emails. However, language barriers can still pose a significant challenge when trying to woo international investors. In this chapter, we explore how ChatGPT can act as your multilingual maestro, facilitating smooth communication.

The Importance of Bridging Language Gaps

LANGUAGE BARRIERS CAN:

- Create misunderstandings that jeopardize deals

- Limit your reach to only those investors who speak your language

- Make you appear less professional or prepared

How ChatGPT Can Help

Instant Translation: ChatGPT can quickly translate key investment documents, emails, or presentations into various languages, although you should always get a professional translation for legal and financial documents.

Cultural Context: ChatGPT can offer tips on cultural norms and etiquette related to business communication in different countries.

Language Training: Want to learn a few phrases to impress a Japanese investor? ChatGPT can provide some basic language lessons.

Real-world Example

SUPPOSE YOU HAVE AN opportunity to pitch to a group of French investors.

Without ChatGPT: You might have to hire a translator, wait for them to translate all your documents, and perhaps even stumble through a pitch meeting with limited French skills.

With ChatGPT: You could have the majority of your documents roughly translated almost instantly, use the bot for real-time email translations, and even learn a few key French phrases to personalize your pitch.

Investing is a global game, and it's not uncommon for startups and growing businesses to seek international investors. However, language barriers can often impede effective communication and make it difficult to capture the attention of investors from different linguistic backgrounds. ChatGPT's real-time translation capabilities can break down these walls, allowing you to communicate your business ideas, goals, and vision seamlessly to a global audience. From pitch presentations to investor communications, using AI for real-time translation can significantly enhance your global outreach.

Tip 1: Pre-Translate Key Materials

BEFORE ENGAGING WITH international investors, use ChatGPT to pre-translate pitch decks, executive summaries, and other key materials into the target language to set a positive first impression.

Tip 2: Localize, Don't Just Translate

LOCALIZATION GOES BEYOND mere translation; it involves adapting your content to the cultural context of your audience. ChatGPT can assist in adapting your messaging to be culturally relevant and sensitive.

Tip 3: Double-check Technical Terminology

INVESTMENT AND FINANCIAL terms can be complex and can have different connotations in different languages. Use ChatGPT to double-check the translation of technical terms to avoid misunderstandings.

Tip 4: Utilize Real-time Features

IN LIVE MEETINGS OR virtual chats, use ChatGPT's real-time translation to ensure smooth communication. This can be particularly beneficial in Q&A sessions.

Tip 5: Test and Iterate

AFTER USING CHATGPT for translation, always test your materials with a native speaker in the target market, if possible. Use their feedback to make necessary adjustments.

By harnessing the power of ChatGPT's real-time translation features, you can reach out to international investors in an effective and linguistically competent manner.

Chapter 25: Automated Risk Assessment Reports

———

The task of conducting risk assessments can be both cumbersome and nerve-wracking. After all, you're trying to identify and evaluate uncertainties that could adversely affect your startup. In this chapter, we'll look at how ChatGPT can be your sidekick in developing automated risk assessment reports that could make you and your investors sleep a little easier.

Why Risk Assessments Matter

INVESTORS WANT TO KNOW they're not throwing their money into a black hole. They need assurances, or at least, well-calculated risks. A comprehensive risk assessment can provide:

- A detailed look at potential risks

- Mitigation strategies

- Contingency plans

How ChatGPT Can Help

Risk Identification: ChatGPT can help brainstorm a list of potential risks based on the nature of your business, market conditions, and other factors.

Mitigation Strategies: Once risks are identified, ChatGPT can assist in crafting mitigation plans.

Automated Reporting: ChatGPT can generate a draft of the risk assessment report, which you can then refine and personalize.

Real-world Example

YOU ARE IN THE RENEWABLE energy sector and face a variety of risks like technology failures, regulatory changes, and natural disasters.

Without ChatGPT: You'd be spending a lot of time gathering data, consulting experts, and manually creating a risk assessment report.

With ChatGPT: You could start by inputting, "List potential risks for a renewable energy startup." Then, follow up with, "Suggest mitigation strategies for technology failure risks." Before you know it, you'll have the skeleton of a risk assessment report ready for fine-tuning.

Risk is an inevitable part of any investment equation, and it's crucial for both startups and investors to understand these risks in detail. Traditional risk assessment can be time-consuming and often requires specialized expertise. However, ChatGPT can help you automate the creation of comprehensive risk assessment reports, which not only save time but also provide a more data-driven approach to evaluating uncertainties. With the help of AI, you can categorize and quantify risks, providing your investors with a thorough understanding of the potential challenges and how you plan to mitigate them.

Tip 1: Keep It Updated

RISKS CAN CHANGE AS your business grows or the market shifts. Use ChatGPT to frequently update your risk assessment reports to reflect the most current data and insights.

Tip 2: Prioritize Risks

NOT ALL RISKS CARRY the same weight. Use ChatGPT to help you identify and prioritize the most significant risks that need immediate attention. This helps in focusing investor discussions on what truly matters.

Tip 3: Pair Risks with Mitigations

WHENEVER YOU PRESENT a risk, also present a mitigation strategy. ChatGPT can help draft these countermeasures efficiently, making your risk assessment report not just a list of problems but a plan for how to overcome them.

Utilizing ChatGPT for automated risk assessment can streamline a cumbersome process and add a layer of sophistication to your investor communications. It positions you as a proactive, transparent entrepreneur who has a grip on the challenges ahead.

Chapter 26: Curating Competitive Analysis Data

―――

Understanding your competition is as essential as understanding your own business when it comes to attracting investors. The landscape of who's who, what they're doing, and how they're performing can make or break your investment pitch. In this chapter, let's dive into how ChatGPT can become your virtual competitive analysis manager.

The Imperative of Competitive Analysis

A WELL-CRAFTED COMPETITIVE analysis can:

• Help you identify your unique value proposition

• Offer insights into market trends

• Enable you to understand the strengths and weaknesses of your competitors

How ChatGPT Can Assist

Data Collection: ChatGPT can't browse the internet in real-time but can help you outline the types of data you should collect about your competitors, including market share, customer reviews, and financial metrics.

SWOT Analysis: You can also use ChatGPT to help create a SWOT (Strengths, Weaknesses, Opportunities, and Threats) analysis for each of your competitors.

Report Generation: ChatGPT can help you draft the competitive analysis report, incorporating all the data and insights you've gathered.

Real-world Example

YOU'RE IN THE ED-TECH sector, and you face stiff competition.

Without ChatGPT: Hours of research, data gathering, and report writing could lie ahead of you, taking precious time away from other tasks.

With ChatGPT: Start with a prompt like, "Outline a competitive analysis report for an ed-tech startup." ChatGPT can guide you through the types of information you should gather, suggest potential sources, and even help draft the report once you have the data.

Understanding your competition is not just beneficial; it's essential for the success of your business. ChatGPT can be a valuable tool for curating and summarizing competitive analysis data, helping you make better-informed decisions and giving your investors a clearer picture of the market landscape. By utilizing AI-powered data scraping and analysis, you can present a well-researched view of the competitors, market trends, and gaps that can be capitalized on.

Tip 1: Use Real-Time Data

WHEN POSSIBLE, SET up ChatGPT to pull in real-time data for your competitive analysis. The business environment is always changing, and up-to-date information can give you a crucial advantage.

Tip 2: Go Beyond Surface Metrics

WHILE IT'S EASY TO focus on obvious metrics like sales or customer base, use ChatGPT to delve deeper into areas like customer satisfaction, innovation, or sustainability practices among competitors.

Tip 3: Comparative Benchmarking

USE CHATGPT TO BENCHMARK your company's performance against your competitors on various parameters. This helps to understand where you stand and what you need to improve.

Tip 4: Visualize Data

TEXT-BASED DATA IS good, but visual representations can be more impactful. Utilize ChatGPT's data visualization capabilities to make graphs or charts that can be easily incorporated into investor presentations.

Tip 5: Keep an Eye on Emerging Competitors

NEW COMPETITORS CAN appear quickly, and their initial impact might be small but significant in the long term. Use ChatGPT to keep track of emerging players in your field.

Chapter 27: Generating Content for Crowdfunding Campaigns

———

Crowdfunding platforms like Kickstarter and Indiegogo have democratized the fundraising landscape, making it possible for entrepreneurs to raise money without traditional investors. But a successful crowdfunding campaign isn't just about having a great idea; it's about communicating that idea effectively. In this chapter, let's explore how ChatGPT can be your creative content partner for a crowdfunding campaign that not only meets but exceeds its funding goals.

The Art of Crowdfunding

A WELL-EXECUTED CROWDFUNDING campaign requires:

- A compelling story

- Clear communication of the problem you're solving

- Transparency about how the funds will be used

How ChatGPT Can Be Your Co-Creator

Narrative Building: ChatGPT can help you draft the story of your startup. The "why" behind your venture can often be as compelling as the "what."

Rewards Description: You can use ChatGPT to write descriptions of the rewards that backers will get, making them irresistible.

Updates and Follow-ups: Regular communication is key to a successful campaign. ChatGPT can assist you in creating update posts and follow-up emails to backers.

Real-world Example

YOU'RE LAUNCHING A tech wearable and need to crowdfund for initial production.

Without ChatGPT: You'd be facing the daunting task of writing, rewriting, and tweaking every single piece of content yourself.

With ChatGPT: You could start by saying, "Help me craft the story of my tech wearable startup for a crowdfunding campaign." ChatGPT will guide you through the storytelling elements that resonate with potential backers, saving you time and creative energy.

Crowdfunding has democratized the fundraising landscape, allowing small startups and individual entrepreneurs to reach a large audience of potential investors and backers. While the concept is compelling, the execution requires careful planning and an array of well-crafted content. ChatGPT can be your partner in creating engaging, clear, and persuasive material for your crowdfunding campaign, from video scripts to FAQ sections and update posts. This ensures your message reaches the right audience, in the right way, at the right time.

Tip 1: Target Audience Analysis

BEFORE YOU START CREATING any content, use ChatGPT to perform a target audience analysis. Tailoring your messaging to meet the needs and expectations of your target demographic can significantly improve the chances of your campaign's success.

Tip 2: A/B Testing

FOR CRUCIAL ELEMENTS like headlines or call-to-actions, use ChatGPT to generate multiple versions. Then, apply A/B testing to see which ones resonate most with your audience.

Tip 3: Storytelling is Key

USE CHATGPT TO HELP you craft a compelling story around your product or service. Storytelling can humanize your brand and create an emotional connection with potential backers.

Tip 4: Update Regularly

CROWDFUNDING CAMPAIGNS often span several weeks or even months. Use ChatGPT to schedule regular updates and content drops to keep the momentum going and your backers engaged.

Tip 5: FAQ Automation

CHATGPT CAN AUTOMATICALLY generate a detailed FAQ section based on common queries in your industry or product category, saving you time and ensuring that you don't miss any essential questions backers may have.

Tip 6: Multi-format Content

USE CHATGPT TO CREATE diverse types of content, including blog posts, social media updates, and email newsletters, to appeal to different segments of your audience.

Tip 7: Social Proof

UTILIZE CHATGPT TO draft testimonials or case studies, enhancing the credibility of your product or campaign.

Tip 8: Monitor and Adapt

CHATGPT CAN ANALYZE comments or questions from backers to identify common themes or concerns. Use this feedback to adapt your campaign in real-time.

Tip 9: Legal Clarity

USE CHATGPT TO GENERATE disclaimers or legal notes that might be needed to make sure your campaign abides by the rules and regulations of the crowdfunding platform and the jurisdiction you operate in.

Tip 10: Post-Campaign Communication

ONCE YOUR CAMPAIGN is over, whether it was successful or not, you need to communicate the outcome to your backers. ChatGPT can assist in crafting these crucial post-campaign messages, which can set the stage for future endeavors.

Chapter 28: Auto-summarizing Investor Feedback

———

Investor feedback is a treasure trove of insights, often helping you see blind spots or opportunities that you may have overlooked. However, sifting through multiple pieces of feedback can be overwhelming. That's where ChatGPT steps in, acting as your personal feedback analyst. In this chapter, we'll delve into how you can make the most of investor feedback through ChatGPT's auto-summarizing capabilities.

The Significance of Investor Feedback

CAPTURING AND INTERPRETING investor feedback can:

- Improve your product or service

- Help you refine your investment pitch

- Give you a better sense of your startup's market positioning

How ChatGPT Can Help

Organizing Feedback: ChatGPT can help you categorize the feedback you receive into various buckets such as product, market fit, financials, and team.

Summarization: Once organized, ChatGPT can assist you in summarizing each category to extract actionable insights.

Plan of Action: You can use ChatGPT to outline a plan based on the summarized feedback, focusing on immediate and long-term actions.

Real-world Example

YOU'VE PITCHED TO SEVERAL investors and have a hodgepodge of feedback notes.

Without ChatGPT: Manually sorting and summarizing these could take hours, possibly days.

With ChatGPT: You can input these notes into a document and ask ChatGPT to summarize feedback under different headers like 'Product,' 'Market,' and 'Financials.'

Feedback from investors is a treasure trove of insights, yet managing, analyzing, and drawing actionable conclusions from it can be a time-consuming endeavor. ChatGPT can streamline this process by auto-summarizing lengthy investor feedback into digestible insights. Whether it's comments on your pitch, suggestions for your business model, or critiques of your product, ChatGPT can help you focus on what truly matters for the betterment of your startup.

Tip 1: Set Context

BEFORE ASKING CHATGPT to summarize feedback, provide it with context. Let the AI know what stage your startup is at, the industry you're in, and what type of investment you're looking for. The more context you provide, the more tailored and relevant the summary will be.

Tip 2: Frequency Matters

REGULARLY UPDATE THE feedback database and let ChatGPT auto-summarize it. Consistent updates will allow you to capture changing investor sentiments and adapt accordingly.

Tip 3: Prioritize Feedback

USE CHATGPT TO HELP you prioritize feedback based on your startup's immediate needs and long-term strategy. Whether it's refining your product or improving your pitch, knowing what to focus on first can make a world of difference.

Tip 4: Tagging and Categorization

IN ADDITION TO SUMMARIZING, ChatGPT can tag or categorize feedback into themes like "Product," "Market Fit," "Business Model," etc. This can help you quickly identify the areas that require the most attention.

Tip 5: Action Plan

ONCE YOU HAVE THE SUMMARIZED and categorized feedback, use ChatGPT to help draft an action plan. The AI can suggest steps based on the feedback themes, which can serve as a roadmap for your team to execute.

Chapter 29: Building an Investment Case Study

<hr/>

C ase studies serve as a compelling narrative of your startup's journey, capturing the essence of the challenges you've faced and the milestones you've achieved. They can be a powerful tool for gaining investor confidence. In this chapter, we'll explore how ChatGPT can help you articulate an impressive case study that can serve as a cornerstone in your investment-seeking activities.

The Power of a Case Study

WELL-CONSTRUCTED CASE studies can:

- Demonstrate your startup's value proposition

- Show the ROI (Return on Investment) convincingly

- Highlight testimonials and success stories

How ChatGPT Can Assist

Structure and Outline: ChatGPT can help you build an initial outline, breaking down the case study into essential parts like the problem, solution, results, and testimonials.

Content Generation: Flesh out each part with rich, engaging content. ChatGPT can help you draft these sections, focusing on the most compelling aspects of your story.

Data Presentation: ChatGPT can guide you in how to articulate data and metrics that support your case. While it can't generate graphs, it can describe what types of graphs or visuals would be most effective.

Real-world Example

YOU HAVE SUCCESSFULLY onboarded a major client who has greatly benefited from your service.

Without ChatGPT: Compiling this into a case study would require hours of work, including interviews, drafting, and editing.

With ChatGPT: You can input raw interview notes, client metrics, and success indicators into a document. Then, ask ChatGPT to help draft a case study based on this information.

An investment case study is an invaluable asset for startups. It provides a deep dive into a successful investment scenario, allowing both the team and potential investors to understand what worked, what didn't, and why. ChatGPT can assist you in compiling and presenting these complex narratives in a coherent and compelling manner. From gathering essential data points to drafting the narrative, and even polishing the final document, ChatGPT serves as an invaluable tool in this crucial activity.

Tip 1: Define Objectives Clearly

BEFORE DIVING INTO creating a case study, define what you hope to achieve with it. Are you trying to attract more investors, build credibility, or provide educational content for your team? Knowing the objectives will guide the content that needs to be included.

Tip 2: Segment Your Data

USE CHATGPT TO HELP segment your performance data into categories such as "Financial Metrics," "Customer Satisfaction," and "Market Reach." This will not only make the data more digestible but also allow for a more organized case study.

Tip 3: Tell a Story

A CASE STUDY IS NOT just a collection of data points; it's a narrative. Use ChatGPT to help craft a compelling story that takes the reader through challenges, solutions, and results. Frame the data within the context of this story for maximum impact.

Tip 4: Validate with Testimonials

CHATGPT CAN HELP YOU integrate testimonials or quotes from key stakeholders, which can significantly enhance the credibility of your case study. Have the AI draft potential questions to ask for testimonials and even auto-generate email requests to collect them.

Tip 5: Review and Refine

ONCE THE DRAFT IS READY, use ChatGPT for a critical review. The AI can point out gaps, suggest areas for improvement, and even help you polish the language to make the case study more compelling.

Chapter 30: Generating Investment Teasers

⸻

T he art of grabbing investor attention lies in the finesse of your investment teaser. This short, snappy document is often your first foot in the door and can make or break an investor's interest in your startup. In this chapter, we will uncover how ChatGPT can aid in crafting a powerful investment teaser that leaves investors wanting more.

Why Investment Teasers Matter

AN IMPACTFUL INVESTMENT teaser can:

- Generate immediate interest

- Summarize your business concisely

- Set the stage for further discussions

The ChatGPT Advantage

Headline Creation: ChatGPT can assist in crafting eye-catching headlines that instantly grab attention.

Content Briefing: For each section of the teaser, whether it's the problem, solution, or business model, ChatGPT can generate concise and engaging content.

Call-to-Action: An investment teaser must end with a compelling call-to-action (CTA). ChatGPT can help you phrase your CTA in a way that urges investors to take the next step.

A Practical Example

YOU NEED TO SEND OUT teasers for an upcoming funding round.

Without ChatGPT: You may spend hours wondering how to condense all your achievements and plans into a one-pager without losing the essence.

With ChatGPT: You can generate an outline and even a full first draft within minutes, which you can then customize and refine.

Creating a captivating investment teaser is critical for piquing the interest of potential investors. The teaser acts as a concise yet intriguing snapshot of your business, designed to entice the reader into wanting to know more. With ChatGPT's versatility in handling text-based tasks, crafting a compelling investment teaser becomes significantly easier. The AI can help condense complex business information into digestible chunks, identify key selling points, and even refine the language to be more persuasive.

Tip 1: Identify Your Unique Value Proposition

YOUR TEASER NEEDS TO immediately make clear what sets your business apart. Use ChatGPT to brainstorm or refine your unique value proposition and place it prominently in the teaser.

Tip 2: Keep it Short and Sweet

AN INVESTMENT TEASER should not be a lengthy document. Use ChatGPT to help you condense your content without losing essential details, aiming for a one-page format if possible.

Tip 3: Use Attention-Grabbing Headlines

CHATGPT CAN GENERATE catchy and relevant headlines that quickly grab attention, encouraging the reader to delve into the rest of the teaser.

Tip 4: Highlight Key Financials

NUMBERS OFTEN SPEAK louder than words. Use ChatGPT to help you select and present key financial data that demonstrates the viability and growth potential of your business.

Tip 5: Include Success Metrics

IN ADDITION TO FINANCIALS, consider including other forms of success metrics. ChatGPT can assist you in identifying which KPIs would be most impactful in your teaser.

Tip 6: Make it Visually Engaging

A GOOD TEASER IS NOT just about text. ChatGPT can suggest the type of visual elements that can enhance your document, like charts, graphs, or images.

Tip 7: Be Clear on the Ask

WHAT DO YOU WANT THE investor to do next? ChatGPT can help you craft a clear and compelling 'call to action' that guides prospective investors on the next steps.

Tip 8: Review for Confidentiality

USE CHATGPT TO REVIEW the document for any sensitive or confidential information that shouldn't be in a teaser. It can help you rewrite sections to be more generalized while still being compelling.

Tip 9: Include Testimonials

IF YOU HAVE QUOTES from satisfied customers or stakeholders, ChatGPT can help you incorporate these in a meaningful way that adds credibility to your teaser.

Tip 10: Multiple Revisions

DON'T HESITATE TO GO through several iterations. ChatGPT can quickly generate revised versions, allowing you to A/B test different approaches and settle on the most effective one.

Chapter 31: Real-time Market Feedback Analysis

In the rapidly changing landscape of entrepreneurship, timing is often as crucial as the idea itself. Keeping your finger on the market's pulse could give you a significant edge. In this chapter, let's discuss how ChatGPT can help you analyze real-time market feedback for making informed decisions, especially when you're seeking investment.

Why Real-time Market Feedback is Vital

QUICK MARKET FEEDBACK allows you to:

- Adapt to changes efficiently

- Make data-driven decisions

- Build investor confidence through agility

Leverage ChatGPT for Market Feedback

Aggregating Feedback: ChatGPT can assist in collecting and categorizing customer reviews, social media mentions, and other types of feedback for easier analysis.

Interpreting Data: While ChatGPT can't understand numbers, it can help you articulate the significance of market feedback data in a way that resonates with investors.

Drafting Reports: After the analysis, you'll need to share the findings, and ChatGPT can help you craft comprehensive yet easy-to-understand reports.

The Real Deal: An Example

SUPPOSE YOU'VE JUST launched a beta version of your product, and feedback is pouring in.

Without ChatGPT: Analyzing this feedback manually is time-consuming and prone to bias.

With ChatGPT: You can quickly generate a structured document that categorizes the feedback into themes like 'Usability,' 'Features,' 'Pricing,' etc., and then dives into qualitative insights.

The landscape of today's fast-paced market requires businesses to be agile, adaptable, and most importantly, in tune with what their customers are saying. Real-time market feedback analysis is vital for adapting to market demands, spotting trends early, and making timely decisions. With ChatGPT, you can set up systems to analyze customer reviews, social media mentions, or survey responses, and quickly generate summaries, trends, or actionable insights. This accelerates the feedback loop, enabling your business to respond more swiftly to market changes.

Tip 1: Integrate with Existing Tools

CHATGPT CAN BE INTEGRATED with data analytics tools or CRM systems you're already using, providing a seamless flow of information that can be instantly analyzed for trends and patterns.

Tip 2: Automate Sentiment Analysis

UTILIZE CHATGPT TO perform sentiment analysis on customer reviews and social media comments. This will allow you to quickly understand the general mood around your product or service and act accordingly.

Tip 3: Prioritize Feedback

NOT ALL FEEDBACK IS created equal. ChatGPT can help you identify the most pressing issues or the most frequent suggestions, allowing you to prioritize what to address first for maximum impact.

Tip 4: Create Alert Systems

CHATGPT CAN ASSIST in setting up automated alert systems for specific keywords or trends. If a particular issue starts to escalate or a positive buzz begins to form, you'll know immediately and can react accordingly.

Tip 5: Act on Insights

ANALYSIS IS ONLY AS good as the actions that follow. ChatGPT can help you draft plans or communications based on the insights gathered, so you can act quickly and effectively.

Chapter 32: Creating Product Demo Scripts

───

Ah, the product demo: that make-or-break moment where your product has to shine brighter than a diamond in a goat's belly. It's often a critical component of pitching to investors. In this chapter, we'll explore how ChatGPT can assist you in writing an impressive product demo script that dazzles your audience.

The Importance of a Good Product Demo

AN EFFECTIVE PRODUCT demo can:

- Convey the uniqueness of your product

- Showcase its capabilities and features

- Build trust and credibility

How ChatGPT Can Help

Outlining the Flow: ChatGPT can help generate an outline that ensures a logical flow from problem identification to the solution your product provides.

Feature Highlighting: When discussing features, ChatGPT can assist in crafting engaging descriptions that emphasize the value proposition.

Engaging Conclusion: A memorable closing statement can make a lasting impression. ChatGPT can assist in crafting a closing that resonates with your audience.

A Handy Example

YOU'RE PREPARING FOR a crucial investor meeting where a product demo is expected.

Without ChatGPT: You might get tangled in the weeds, overemphasizing features and losing sight of the overall value proposition.

With ChatGPT: Generate a draft script that focuses on the critical aspects of your product, then tailor it to perfection.

Creating a product demo script is an art and a science. It's not just about showcasing the features of your product; it's also about connecting those features to the needs and wants of your target audience. By employing ChatGPT, you can draft compelling narratives that highlight the problems your product solves while also customizing the content to appeal to various investor personas. This blend of tailored messaging and technical detail ensures your demo not only informs but also impresses.

Tip 1: Start with an Outline

BEFORE DIVING INTO the script, create an outline to structure the flow of your demo. ChatGPT can assist in generating a logical framework, ensuring all essential points are covered.

Tip 2: Use Storytelling Techniques

INCORPORATE STORYTELLING into your script to make the demo more engaging. ChatGPT can help in crafting anecdotes or customer scenarios that highlight the benefits of your product.

Tip 3: Focus on Benefits, Not Just Features

WHILE IT'S IMPORTANT to showcase what your product can do, investors are more interested in how it solves a problem or fulfills a need. ChatGPT can help you articulate these benefits clearly in your script.

Tip 4: Address Possible Objections

CHATGPT CAN HELP YOU anticipate and address potential objections or questions investors may have. This will make your demo come across as thorough and well-thought-out.

Tip 5: Keep it Concise but Complete

LESS IS OFTEN MORE. While it's tempting to include every minor feature or detail, focus on the most compelling aspects of your product. ChatGPT can assist in creating a script that's concise yet comprehensive.

Mastering the art of the product demo script can significantly impact your ability to attract investment and win over stakeholders.

Chapter 33: Designing Investor Polls and Surveys

———

I n the world of investment, the voice of your stakeholders matters. What better way to gauge what they're thinking than through well-crafted polls and surveys? This chapter will enlighten you on how to use ChatGPT to design polls and surveys that capture investors' perceptions, preferences, and pain points.

Why Investor Polls and Surveys?

INVESTOR POLLS AND surveys help:

- Understand investor sentiment

- Gauge interest in new features or directions

- Collect actionable feedback for improvement

How ChatGPT Can Help

Question Design: ChatGPT can help generate relevant and unbiased questions that elicit meaningful responses.

Survey Structure: A well-designed survey has a logical flow. ChatGPT can assist in outlining the survey structure for optimal engagement.

Analysis: After the survey is completed, ChatGPT can help summarize the results in a digestible format suitable for presentations or reports.

A Mini Case-Study

IMAGINE YOU'RE PONDERING over launching a new feature and want to know what your investors think.

Without ChatGPT: You might create a less-than-perfect survey that fails to capture nuances, thereby missing crucial insights.

With ChatGPT: Generate a survey with precise questions that capture a range of responses, making the analysis more insightful.

Gathering investor feedback is crucial for adapting your business strategy, tweaking your pitch, and even for product development. Polls and surveys provide a structured way to capture this invaluable input. Using ChatGPT can significantly ease the process of designing these feedback tools. From generating insightful questions to customizing question formats, ChatGPT can help you create polls and surveys that yield actionable insights.

Tip 1: Know Your Objective

BEFORE YOU CREATE A poll or survey, be clear on what you want to achieve. ChatGPT can help you articulate your objectives and even suggest types of questions that align with your goals.

Tip 2: Segment Your Audience

TAILOR YOUR QUESTIONS to different types of investors. With ChatGPT, you can easily customize your survey for various groups, from angel investors to venture capitalists.

Tip 3: Use a Mix of Question Types

CHATGPT CAN GENERATE a variety of question types—from multiple-choice to Likert scales—to keep respondents engaged and provide you with a range of insights.

Tip 4: Keep It Short and Sweet

INVESTORS ARE BUSY people. ChatGPT can help you design a concise yet comprehensive survey that respects your respondents' time while still gathering the information you need.

Tip 5: Test Before You Send

ALWAYS PILOT YOUR SURVEY on a smaller group before sending it out widely. ChatGPT can assist in evaluating the effectiveness of your questions and suggest improvements.

By leveraging ChatGPT's capabilities in question generation and customization, you can design investor polls and surveys that not only capture essential data but also enhance your relationship with your stakeholders.

Chapter 34: Fine-tuning Your Unique Value Proposition

———

Your Unique Value Proposition (UVP) is your golden ticket in the investor circus. It succinctly states why your product or service is different and why that difference matters. This chapter will guide you on how to fine-tune your UVP using ChatGPT.

The Magic of a Strong UVP

A COMPELLING UVP CAN:

- Set you apart from the competition

- Make your pitch more memorable

- Drive investment decisions in your favor

How ChatGPT Can Help

Idea Generation: ChatGPT can assist in brainstorming various angles for your UVP. Sometimes, all it takes is a fresh perspective.

Refinement: A good UVP is clear, concise, and compelling. ChatGPT can help refine your statements to meet these criteria.

Stakeholder-Specific Adjustments: Different stakeholders may require a different focus. ChatGPT can help tailor your UVP for various audiences, including investors.

Real-world Scenario

LET'S SAY YOU'VE GOT a sustainable energy startup.

Without ChatGPT: Your UVP might be as dull as dishwater, like "We make renewable energy."

With ChatGPT: Transform it into something snazzier, such as "Empowering a greener tomorrow through innovative, cost-effective renewable energy solutions."

Your Unique Value Proposition (UVP) serves as your business's elevator pitch to investors and can make or break their decision to invest in your startup. ChatGPT can help refine your UVP, ensuring that it is concise, relevant, and compelling. It can assist in wording, structure, and even in conducting a mini-SWOT analysis to ensure that your UVP stands out in a crowded market.

Tip 1: Focus on the Benefit, Not Just Features

REMEMBER THAT YOUR UVP is not just about what your product does, but what problem it solves. ChatGPT can help you phrase your UVP in a way that emphasizes the benefits to the customer.

Tip 2: Use Simple, Direct Language

INVESTORS DON'T HAVE time to wade through jargon or complex sentences. ChatGPT can help you refine your UVP into simple and direct language that communicates your message effectively.

Tip 3: Test Multiple Versions

DON'T SETTLE FOR THE first draft. Use ChatGPT to create multiple versions of your UVP and test them with a small audience to see which one resonates the most.

Tip 4: Align With Your Brand

YOUR UVP SHOULD BE consistent with your brand's tone and messaging. ChatGPT can help ensure that your UVP aligns well with your overall brand strategy.

Tip 5: Quantify When Possible

IF YOU HAVE METRICS or data to back up your claims, include them in your UVP. ChatGPT can help you integrate these numbers smoothly into your proposition, making it more persuasive.

By applying these tips and using ChatGPT as a resource, you can create a UVP that not only captivates your target investors but also gives you a competitive edge.

Chapter 35: Preparing for Q&A in Investor Meetings

———

The question-and-answer session in investor meetings can make or break your pitch. The audience's queries can range from financials to future plans and everything in-between. How do you prepare for such a barrage? This chapter will explore how ChatGPT can assist you in getting ready for investor Q&As.

Why Q&A Prep Is Crucial

BEING UNPREPARED FOR a Q&A session can:

- Damage your credibility

- Lower investor confidence

- Miss out on securing crucial investment

How ChatGPT Can Help

Question Repository: ChatGPT can help create a comprehensive list of potential questions you might face, based on the industry and the nature of your business.

Scripted Responses: Generate well-articulated, concise answers to common questions, so you're never caught off guard.

Mock Q&A: Use ChatGPT to conduct a simulated Q&A session, helping you refine your responses and timing.

Case Example

LET'S ASSUME YOUR STARTUP is in the health tech sector.

Without ChatGPT: You might be stumped by a question about HIPAA compliance or scalability.

With ChatGPT: You'll have prepared answers, allowing you to appear knowledgeable and in control, boosting investor confidence.

The Q&A session in an investor meeting is your opportunity to demonstrate the depth of your knowledge and the viability of your startup. Often, this is where investors make their final assessment about your investment-worthiness. ChatGPT can be an invaluable tool in your preparation, helping you anticipate questions, refine your answers, and even simulate a Q&A session to ensure you're thoroughly prepared.

Tip 1: Anticipate Tough Questions

THINK ABOUT THE HARDEST questions you could be asked and prepare your answers in advance. ChatGPT can help by generating a list of potential questions based on your business model, industry, and common investor concerns.

Tip 2: Be Honest but Positive

IF YOU DON'T KNOW THE answer to a question, it's better to admit it than to bluff. ChatGPT can assist in framing your honest response in a way that still portrays you and your startup in a positive light.

Tip 3: Rehearse Your Answers

USE CHATGPT TO SIMULATE a Q&A session. The more you practice, the more confident and articulate you will be during the actual meeting.

Tip 4: Align Your Answers with Your Business Plan

ENSURE THAT YOUR ANSWERS in the Q&A session are consistent with the information in your business plan. ChatGPT can help you cross-reference your answers for consistency.

Tip 5: Address the Financials

INVESTORS ARE LIKELY to probe into your financial assumptions, revenue model, and more. Use ChatGPT to help you prepare comprehensive answers about your financial metrics.

Tip 6: Show Team Strengths

YOUR TEAM IS A CRITICAL part of your startup's success. Be prepared to talk about your team's skills and experience. ChatGPT can help you articulate these points effectively.

Tip 7: Keep Answers Concise

INVESTORS APPRECIATE brevity. ChatGPT can help you condense complex explanations into concise, understandable answers.

Tip 8: Control the Room

INVESTOR MEETINGS CAN go off on tangents. Use ChatGPT to prepare transitional phrases and redirecting questions to keep the focus on your startup's strengths and opportunities.

By incorporating these tips and using ChatGPT as part of your preparation, you'll be better equipped to navigate the crucial Q&A session in your investor meetings.

Chapter 36: Personalized Investor Updates

———

Investors are not just faceless entities; they're people who have put their faith and resources into your venture. They love nothing more than being in the know. A generic quarterly report? Nah, let's add a personal touch. Here's how ChatGPT can assist you in personalizing investor updates.

The Importance of Personal Touch

PERSONALIZED UPDATES can:

- Strengthen the investor-founder relationship

- Increase investor engagement

- Lead to future investments or beneficial introductions

How ChatGPT Can Help

Data Integration: ChatGPT can pull together various data points on your business's performance and condense them into digestible formats, ready for personalization.

Segmentation: Use ChatGPT to create distinct categories of investors—such as angel investors, venture capitalists, and family funds—and craft messages tailored to each group.

Automated yet Personal: ChatGPT can help you draft updates that, while automated, feel deeply personal and engaging.

Real-world Scenario

IMAGINE YOU'VE SECURED funding from a mix of venture capitalists and angel investors.

Without ChatGPT: You send out a one-size-fits-all update, which reads like a monotonous annual report.

With ChatGPT: You send tailored updates that resonate with each investor type, making them feel seen and valued.

Staying in regular contact with your investors is crucial for building and maintaining strong relationships. Personalized updates are a transparent way to keep your investors informed about your business's progress, challenges, and future plans. With the help of ChatGPT, you can generate customized, insightful, and well-crafted updates quickly, allowing you to focus more on running your business.

Tip 1: Set a Consistent Schedule

CONSISTENCY IS KEY when it comes to investor updates. Use ChatGPT to set reminders or even to auto-generate drafts for monthly or quarterly updates.

Tip 2: Include Key Performance Indicators (KPIs)

INVESTORS WANT TO SEE measurable growth and improvement. ChatGPT can help you articulate and visualize your KPIs effectively in the updates, ensuring that the data you present is both accurate and compelling.

Tip 3: Discuss Challenges and Solutions

TRANSPARENCY BUILDS trust. Use ChatGPT to help you frame challenges in a way that shows you are aware of them and are taking steps to address them.

Tip 4: Tailor the Content

DIFFERENT INVESTORS may be interested in different aspects of your business. Use ChatGPT to help customize the investor updates according to the preferences and concerns of each investor.

Tip 5: Include a Call-to-Action

WHETHER IT'S A REQUEST for introductions to potential customers or feedback on a new feature, a call-to-action engages your investors. ChatGPT can suggest appropriate calls-to-action based on the content of your update.

Tip 6: Add a Personal Touch

INVESTORS INVEST IN people as much as they do in businesses. Use ChatGPT to inject a bit of your personality or the team's culture into the updates, making them more relatable and engaging.By following these tips and using ChatGPT to aid you in crafting your updates, you'll be well on your way to building stronger, more transparent relationships with your investors.

Chapter 37: Writing Award Applications for Start-up Competitions

―――

Applying for start-up competitions can be a great way to garner attention, win cash prizes, or even secure investment. However, the application process can be time-consuming and require a knack for persuasive writing. Enter ChatGPT, your trusty sidekick in crafting compelling applications.

Why Bother with Competitions?

PARTICIPATING IN COMPETITIONS can:

- Provide significant media exposure

- Validate your business idea

- Help you network with industry professionals

How ChatGPT Can Assist

Strategic Content: ChatGPT can help you identify the unique selling points (USPs) of your start-up and articulate them compellingly in the application.

Narrative Crafting: The AI can guide you in creating a story around your start-up, making your application more engaging.

Fine-tuning: Use ChatGPT to iterate and refine your application, improving its clarity and impact.

A Real-life Example

LET'S ASSUME YOU'VE just heard about a prestigious start-up competition focused on sustainability.

Without ChatGPT: You might scribble down some key points, but the narrative lacks coherence, and you miss the deadline.

With ChatGPT: The AI helps you create a cohesive, compelling application, well before the deadline, increasing your chances of catching the judges' attention.

Entering start-up competitions can provide your business with valuable exposure, potential funding, and networking opportunities. The application process often requires a well-articulated vision, a compelling business plan, and clear answers to a variety of questions. ChatGPT can assist in drafting and refining these crucial elements, allowing you to present your start-up in the best light possible.

Tip 1: Understand the Criteria

BEFORE YOU BEGIN WRITING, use ChatGPT to help you research and summarize the competition's criteria and guidelines. This ensures that your application is tailored and relevant.

Tip 2: Be Concise but Comprehensive

SPACE IS OFTEN LIMITED on application forms. ChatGPT can help you to be concise without sacrificing essential details, making every word count.

Tip 3: Use Storytelling

INVESTORS AND JUDGES love a good story. Use ChatGPT to help you weave your business facts and figures into a compelling narrative that captures attention.

Tip 4: Proofread Multiple Times

A SINGLE MISTAKE CAN make a poor impression. Utilize ChatGPT's capabilities to help proofread your application for grammatical errors and inconsistencies.

Tip 5: Leverage Testimonials

IF THE COMPETITION allows for it, include customer testimonials to validate your business. ChatGPT can help you draft and format these effectively.

By applying these tips and employing ChatGPT in your application process, you stand a greater chance of capturing the judges' attention and perhaps even taking home the grand prize

Chapter 38: Drafting Public and Shareholder Statements

P ublic and shareholder statements are critical in conveying the position and progress of a company. A well-crafted statement can inspire confidence, while a poorly composed one can create unnecessary chaos. With ChatGPT, drafting clear and effective statements just got easier.

The Art of Diplomacy

PUBLIC AND SHAREHOLDER statements often require:

- A delicate balance of transparency and discretion

- Clear messaging to align stakeholders

- Diplomacy to manage sensitive issues

How ChatGPT Can Help

Message Clarity: ChatGPT can help you sift through jargon and focus on creating straightforward, comprehensible statements.

Tone Matching: With its ability to analyze and replicate tone, ChatGPT can ensure your public statements are aligned with your corporate identity.

Legal Lingo: ChatGPT can assist in including the necessary disclaimers or legal terms, making your statements more robust.

Case Scenario

SUPPOSE YOUR COMPANY has just experienced a major setback, like a data breach.

Without ChatGPT: A hastily written public statement might confuse shareholders and the public, leading to a loss of trust.

With ChatGPT: Your statement is clear, responsible, and well-thought-out, which can go a long way in damage control.

Transparency and clear communication are key when it comes to public and shareholder statements. These documents can affect your company's reputation, stock price, and stakeholder trust. ChatGPT can be an invaluable tool for drafting, revising, and fine-tuning these crucial pieces of communication, ensuring they are accurate, concise, and impactful.

Tip 1: Prioritize Clarity

AVOID JARGON AND COMPLEX language when drafting statements. Use ChatGPT to convert complex financial data into easily understandable language for your shareholders and the general public.

Tip 2: Stay Consistent

CONSISTENCY IN TONE, language, and formatting is crucial. ChatGPT can help you maintain this consistency across all your public and shareholder communications.

Tip 3: Legal Review is Essential

BEFORE PUBLISHING ANY statement, make sure it has been reviewed for legal compliance. While ChatGPT can assist in the initial drafting, always consult with legal experts to ensure you're not inadvertently making commitments or disclosures that could be problematic.

Tip 4: Timeliness is Key

IN TODAY'S FAST-PACED world, delayed communication can lead to speculation and rumors. Use ChatGPT to quickly draft statements that address issues or news affecting your company in real-time.

Tip 5: Reiterate Core Values

EVERY PUBLIC OR SHAREHOLDER statement is an opportunity to reiterate your company's core values and mission. ChatGPT can help you seamlessly integrate these elements into your communication.

By utilizing these tips and leveraging the capabilities of ChatGPT, you can ensure that your public and shareholder statements are not just informative, but also reinforce the credibility and trustworthiness of your company.

Chapter 39: Tracking and Reporting Key Performance Indicators (KPIs)

⸻

K ey Performance Indicators (KPIs) serve as the North Star for any organization, guiding your progress and revealing areas for improvement. While it's one thing to identify your KPIs, it's another to effectively track and communicate them, especially to investors. This is where ChatGPT shines.

Why KPIs Matter to Investors

INVESTORS LOVE NUMBERS and metrics that show:

- The health and scalability of your business

- Your ability to meet and exceed targets

- The effectiveness of your team

How ChatGPT Can Assist

Dashboard Creation: Use ChatGPT to draft content for your KPI dashboards, adding descriptive texts and insights to help investors understand the metrics.

Trend Analysis: ChatGPT can help you script a narrative around your KPIs, discussing trends and explaining fluctuations in performance.

Investor Reports: Use ChatGPT to help outline and draft your quarterly or annual investor reports, ensuring all important KPIs are highlighted and explained.

Case Study

IMAGINE YOUR COMPANY has shown a 20% growth in customer retention but a 5% decline in new user acquisition.

Without ChatGPT: You might provide the data, but the story behind the numbers remains unclear.

With ChatGPT: The AI helps you articulate the actions taken to improve retention and provides a reasoned analysis of the decline in new user acquisition.

Key Performance Indicators are the backbone of any performance-driven organization. They provide valuable metrics that inform decision-making processes and guide future strategies. ChatGPT can be a crucial aid in tracking, analyzing, and reporting these KPIs, freeing up human resources for more complex tasks and ensuring a more streamlined, error-free reporting process.

Tip 1: Define Your KPIs Clearly

BEFORE YOU CAN TRACK anything, you need to know what you're tracking. Use ChatGPT to help consolidate the most important metrics for your organization and ensure they are communicated clearly to your team.

Tip 2: Automate Regular Updates

CHATGPT CAN HELP IN automating the process of pulling the latest numbers and preparing KPI reports. This ensures timely availability of crucial data for key stakeholders.

Tip 3: Visualize the Data

A PICTURE IS WORTH a thousand words. Use ChatGPT in conjunction with data visualization tools to create compelling dashboards that make the data easy to understand at a glance.

Tip 4: Compare and Contrast

CHATGPT CAN ASSIST in compiling comparative data that puts your KPIs in the context of past performance, industry benchmarks, or competitor data. This makes the insights more actionable.

Tip 5: Don't Overlook the Narrative

WHILE NUMBERS ARE IMPORTANT, the story they tell is crucial. ChatGPT can help craft the narrative around the KPIs, providing explanations, highlights, and focus areas that are easy for stakeholders to digest.

In the next chapter, we will delve into how ChatGPT can assist in training team members on financial terminology, ensuring everyone in your organization is well-equipped to understand and act on the KPIs you are tracking.

Chapter 40: Training Team Members on Financial Terminology

In a startup or any growing business, not everyone is a financial whiz. However, when it comes to investor interactions or internal decision-making, a baseline understanding of financial jargon is invaluable. ChatGPT can serve as your team's virtual financial tutor.

Why Financial Literacy Matters

A TEAM THAT UNDERSTANDS financial terms can:

- Make informed decisions

- Collaborate effectively with different departments

- Better prepare for investor interactions

How ChatGPT Can Help

Glossary Creation: ChatGPT can compile a comprehensive glossary of financial terms tailored to your industry, making it easier for team members to get up to speed.

Quizzes and Tests: Use ChatGPT to generate quizzes that test your team's understanding of financial terms, ensuring they are well-prepared for investor meetings.

Scenario-based Training: ChatGPT can craft hypothetical financial scenarios for role-playing exercises, allowing your team to practice decision-making based on financial data.

Case Example

SAY YOUR MARKETING and Finance departments are not on the same page regarding the term "Customer Lifetime Value."

Without ChatGPT: Meetings are more time-consuming due to the need for explanations and clarifications.

With ChatGPT: A quick tutorial or quiz generated by ChatGPT can get everyone on the same page, saving time and reducing misunderstandings.

Financial literacy is a key skill that is often overlooked but crucial for the success of a business. Having a team that understands the basic financial terms and metrics can lead to more informed decisions and a more cohesive working environment. ChatGPT can be an invaluable tool for on-the-fly training, offering concise explanations and even interactive scenarios to help team members grasp complex financial terms.

Tip 1: Start with Basics

BEFORE DIVING INTO complex financial jargon, use ChatGPT to provide team members with the basic terms that are commonly used in your industry. This will form the foundation upon which more advanced concepts can be built.

Tip 2: Make it Interactive

FINANCIAL LEARNING doesn't have to be boring. Use ChatGPT to create interactive quizzes or flashcards that team members can engage with, helping to reinforce learning and retention.

Tip 3: Contextualize the Terms

FINANCIAL TERMS CAN be abstract and difficult to understand without context. ChatGPT can provide real-world examples or company-specific scenarios where these terms are applied, making it easier for your team to understand their practical use.

Tip 4: Use Analogies

SOMETIMES COMPLEX FINANCIAL terms can be understood more easily when compared with everyday concepts. ChatGPT can help craft these analogies, offering an alternative explanation that might resonate more with some team members.

Tip 5: Reinforce Regularly

CONSISTENT REINFORCEMENT is key to retention. Use ChatGPT to send out periodic reminders or mini-quizzes to your team, ensuring that their understanding of financial terminology remains fresh and up-to-date.

Chapter 41: Creating a Repository of Potential Investor Questions

———

I nvestor meetings can be unpredictable, with questions ranging from straightforward to left-field. Being prepared for these questions is crucial for securing investment. Here's how ChatGPT can assist you in crafting a repository of potential investor questions.

The Importance of Preparedness

INVESTORS SCRUTINIZE every facet of your business. Being well-prepared:

- Demonstrates your mastery of the business.

- Builds investor confidence.

- Allows you to control the narrative.

How ChatGPT Can Assist

Question Generation: ChatGPT can brainstorm a comprehensive list of questions that investors might ask. These can range from financial queries to questions about your team, technology, and market fit.

Answer Templates: Once you have a list of questions, ChatGPT can help you draft succinct and persuasive answers.

Regular Updates: As your business evolves, new questions may arise. ChatGPT can help you regularly update your repository with fresh questions and answers.

Practical Example

IMAGINE YOUR BUSINESS has just launched a new product line.

Without ChatGPT: You're on the defensive, reacting to questions rather than driving the conversation.

With ChatGPT: Your repository equips you with pre-prepared answers to a variety of questions, allowing you to steer the conversation proactively.

Investor interactions can be unpredictable, but being prepared for any curveball questions can provide you with an invaluable advantage. ChatGPT is not just a tool for generating content; it can also be your virtual "sparring partner," helping you to compile a comprehensive list of tough questions you might face from investors. This repository will not only prepare you for the actual meetings but also help you refine your business model, ensuring that you've considered every angle.

Tip 1: Prioritize High-Impact Questions

USE CHATGPT TO GENERATE questions that are most likely to be asked by investors focused on your industry. Prioritizing these questions will help you spend your preparation time more effectively.

Tip 2: Organize by Category

ONCE YOU HAVE A LIST of potential questions, use ChatGPT to help you categorize them based on topics such as Financials, Team,

Product, Market, and so on. This will make it easier for you to prepare targeted responses.

Tip 3: Simulate Investor Meetings

PRACTICE MAKES PERFECT. Use ChatGPT to role-play as an investor, throwing these challenging questions at you in a simulated setting. This will help you refine your answers and improve your confidence.

Tip 4: Update Regularly

THE INVESTMENT LANDSCAPE and your business are always evolving. Make it a practice to revisit and update your repository periodically. ChatGPT can help by suggesting new questions that may have become relevant.

Tip 5: Include Red Flags

HAVE CHATGPT HELP YOU identify potential "red flag" questions that could indicate critical concerns from investors. Preparing strong answers for these can make or break your pitch.

5 Tough Investor Questions:

How do you plan to achieve profitability with such high operational costs?

Can you explain the key assumptions behind your financial projections and how you validated them?

Your market is highly competitive. What prevents a bigger player from dominating?

How do you justify your valuation, especially when similar companies in the industry are valued much lower?

If you're not first to market, what is your strategy for capturing market share?

Chapter 42: Scripting Podcasts or Webinars for Investors

───

The podcast and webinar formats have become increasingly popular as means of conveying complex information in a digestible manner. For startups seeking investment, this is a golden opportunity to inform and impress potential investors. ChatGPT can help you produce stellar content that resonates with your target audience.

The Modern Investor's Toolkit

TODAY'S INVESTORS ARE savvy and well-informed, often turning to podcasts and webinars to understand market trends, investment opportunities, and the latest tech advancements. Leveraging these formats can:

- Establish your startup as a thought leader.

- Offer a deeper dive into your company's value proposition.

- Serve as long-lasting content that continues to attract interest over time.

How ChatGPT Can Help

Topic Ideation: ChatGPT can brainstorm potential podcast or webinar topics that align with your startup's mission and resonate with investors.

Script Writing: ChatGPT can help you draft a compelling script, ensuring you cover all the key points in an engaging manner.

Audience Engagement: Use ChatGPT to create interactive segments, such as audience polls or Q&A sessions, to keep investors engaged throughout the podcast or webinar.

Real-world Scenario

LET'S SAY YOU'RE A cleantech startup looking to attract green investors.

Without ChatGPT: You might struggle with choosing the right topic or miss out on important points.

With ChatGPT: Your well-scripted, topic-focused webinar showcases your startup's environmental impact and scalability, captivating your investor audience.

Engaging investors requires more than just sending emails or distributing press releases. Podcasts and webinars offer an excellent medium to present your business's nuances in an engaging and informative manner. With ChatGPT, you can easily script the entire program, ensuring that you communicate clearly, focus on high-impact topics, and leave a lasting impression on potential investors. This format allows you to share your passion, explain complex topics, and answer questions in a more interactive way.

Tip 1: Start with a Strong Hook

YOUR OPENING SHOULD grab attention immediately. Use ChatGPT to generate a compelling introduction that sets the stage and makes listeners want to stay tuned.

Tip 2: Structure for Accessibility

THE SCRIPT SHOULD BE structured so that listeners can easily follow along. Use ChatGPT to create section headers and transitions, making your podcast or webinar easy to understand and more engaging.

Tip 3: Incorporate Interactive Elements

IF YOUR PLATFORM ALLOWS, include polls or Q&A segments in your webinar. ChatGPT can help script these interactive portions to keep your audience engaged and gather valuable feedback.

Tip 4: Rehearse with ChatGPT

BEFORE GOING LIVE, run through your script multiple times. ChatGPT can even help you simulate audience questions or interruptions to better prepare you for the real thing.

Tip 5: Include a Call-to-Action

DON'T FORGET TO DIRECT your audience on what they should do next. Whether it's visiting your website, signing up for a newsletter, or scheduling a meeting, ChatGPT can help you craft a compelling call-to-action.

Chapter 43: Crafting Social Media Announcements for Funding Rounds

———

I n our digital age, social media is more than a platform for selfies and memes; it's a powerful tool for business communication. When your startup secures funding, announcing it effectively on social media can amplify your success. This is where ChatGPT comes into play.

Why Social Media Matters in Funding Announcements

● Visibility: Funding news can catch fire on social media, attracting even more investors, customers, and partners.

● Credibility: Announcing your funding round adds a layer of credibility and induces a sense of FOMO (Fear of Missing Out) among other potential investors.

● Engagement: The interactive nature of social media allows you to gauge reactions, answer questions, and cultivate relationships with investors.

How ChatGPT Can Help

Strategic Phrasing: ChatGPT can help craft an announcement that is compelling and captures the essence of your achievement.

Multiple Formats: ChatGPT can produce text for tweets, LinkedIn posts, and even short video script outlines for platforms like Instagram and TikTok.

Follow-Up Content: The assistant can help design a series of follow-up posts to keep the momentum going, such as behind-the-scenes looks or thank-you notes to investors and team members.

Case in Point

IMAGINE YOUR FINTECH startup just closed a Series B round.

Without ChatGPT: You might end up with a drab, generic announcement that fails to create a buzz.

With ChatGPT: You unveil a punchy, well-crafted social media blitz that not only celebrates your milestone but also intrigues and engages potential investors.

In the modern age of technology, social media is not just a platform for personal updates and memes—it's a vital business tool. Announcing funding rounds on social platforms can be an effective way to reach a broad audience and instill confidence in both current and potential investors. ChatGPT can assist in crafting concise, compelling, and shareable social media announcements, ensuring you say the right things in the right way.

Tip 1: Keep It Short but Impactful

SOCIAL MEDIA IS A PLATFORM where brevity shines. Use ChatGPT to help you distill your message into its most potent form. Aim to catch attention and provoke interest in as few words as possible.

Tip 2: Use Visuals

IMAGES OR VIDEOS CAN make your announcement stand out in a crowded social media feed. ChatGPT can help you draft scripts for brief explainer videos or captions that complement your visuals.

Tip 3: Be Mindful of the Platform

DIFFERENT SOCIAL MEDIA platforms have different audiences and conventions. ChatGPT can customize your message to fit the tone and limitations (like character count) of each platform, be it LinkedIn, Twitter, or Instagram.

Tip 4: Engage with Followers

ONCE YOUR ANNOUNCEMENT is live, there will likely be comments, shares, or mentions. ChatGPT can auto-generate responses to common questions or congratulations to help keep the conversation going.

Tip 5: Measure and Adapt

AFTER YOUR ANNOUNCEMENT, use analytics to gauge its impact. ChatGPT can help you draft follow-up messages or tweak your future social media strategy based on these insights.

Chapter 44: Writing Thank-You Notes to Investors

The art of saying 'thank you' is often underestimated, but in the startup world, it can make all the difference. A well-crafted thank-you note is an excellent opportunity to make a lasting impression on your investors. Here's where ChatGPT can play an important role.

The Significance of Saying Thanks

• Personal Touch: A thoughtful thank-you note adds a personal touch to your professional relationship.

• Strengthen Bonds: It creates an emotional connection, strengthening the bond between you and your investors.

• Future Engagement: A simple thank-you can pave the way for future interactions and investment rounds.

How ChatGPT Can Assist

Tailored Messages: ChatGPT can generate personalized thank-you notes, which could be adapted for each investor, based on the type and level of their involvement.

Reminder System: It can set up a schedule for sending these messages, ensuring you don't forget this crucial step in maintaining investor relations.

Follow-Up Suggestions: ChatGPT can even recommend a strategy for future interactions based on investor responses.

A Real-world Example

YOUR AI-DRIVEN HEALTHCARE startup just received seed funding.

Without ChatGPT: You might send a generic email thanking your investors, which could get lost among dozens of similar messages.

With ChatGPT: A heartwarming, tailored thank-you note arrives in your investors' inboxes, resonating emotionally and setting the stage for future dialogues.

Acknowledging your investors is an essential aspect of maintaining strong business relationships. It's not just a courtesy but a subtle way to keep lines of communication open and foster long-term trust. A personalized, well-crafted thank-you note can go a long way in making your investors feel valued and appreciated. ChatGPT can aid in generating heartfelt thank-you notes that go beyond simple platitudes to genuinely connect with your investors.

Tip 1: Make It Personal

GENERIC THANK-YOU NOTES can often feel impersonal and rushed. Use ChatGPT to help generate specific points of gratitude or tailored messages that can resonate with individual investors.

Tip 2: Be Timely

THE IMPACT OF A THANK-you note diminishes the longer you wait to send it. Use ChatGPT to draft and send these messages as soon as possible after an investment has been made or a milestone reached that involved investor support.

Tip 3: Refer to Future Collaboration

A THANK-YOU NOTE CAN be an opportunity to subtly remind investors about the long-term vision or upcoming milestones. ChatGPT can assist in phrasing this in a way that's exciting but not over-promising.

Tip 4: Include Updates or Milestones

TAKE THIS OPPORTUNITY to provide brief updates or mention milestones that have recently been met. It reassures investors that their money is being put to good use.

Tip 5: Keep the Door Open

CLOSE THE NOTE BY INVITING further dialogue or questions. ChatGPT can help you draft a closing that encourages continued engagement without seeming desperate or overly forward.

Chapter 45: Legal Document Preliminary Reviews

––––

Navigating the labyrinthine world of legal documents can be daunting, especially when you're focused on innovation and growth. Investors require an array of legal agreements, each fraught with legalese that can trip up even the most diligent entrepreneur. This is where ChatGPT can offer some preliminary assistance.

Why Legal Documents Matter

● Trust Building: Transparent and legally sound documents lay the groundwork for trust between you and your investors.

● Risk Mitigation: A well-prepared document minimizes risks and protects both parties' interests.

● Deal Acceleration: Streamlining the review process can speed up investment rounds and get you back to what you do best—building your business.

How ChatGPT Can Help

Initial Scan: While not a substitute for a legal advisor, ChatGPT can scan documents for glaring issues or inconsistencies that need attention.

Terminology Decoding: ChatGPT can help translate legal jargon into plain English, giving you a clearer understanding of the document's contents.

Drafting Aids: For simple agreements or templates, ChatGPT can help in drafting clauses or sections that are standard, saving you time and legal fees.

Real-world Example

LET'S SAY YOUR RENEWABLE energy startup is preparing for Series A funding.

Without ChatGPT: You spend sleepless nights going over legal documents, unsure if you've missed some hidden clause that could come back to haunt you.

With ChatGPT: You get a preliminary review that highlights areas for attention, so when you sit down with your legal team, you're better prepared and the process moves faster.

Legal documentation forms the bedrock of any investment or business transaction. While legal counsel is irreplaceable for the intricacies of legal compliance and contract negotiation, ChatGPT can assist in the preliminary stages of document review. By generating drafts, summarizing complex clauses, or even flagging inconsistent terminology, this tool can make the review process more efficient and less prone to human error.

Tip 1: Use ChatGPT for Initial Drafts

CHATGPT CAN GENERATE drafts of standard legal documents, such as NDAs or term sheets, which you can later refine with your legal team.

Tip 2: Summary Generation

UTILIZE CHATGPT TO summarize key points of complex legal documents, providing a more manageable overview before delving into the details.

Tip 3: Consistency Checks

CHATGPT CAN BE PROGRAMMED to look for inconsistent terminology across different sections of a document, helping to flag potential issues.

Tip 4: Quick Legal Jargon Translation

CHATGPT CAN QUICKLY translate legalese into plain English, making these documents more accessible for team members who aren't legally trained.

Tip 5: Cross-reference Agreements

USE CHATGPT TO CROSS-reference clauses in different agreements to ensure they are consistent and compatible.

Tip 6: Regular Updates

LEGAL LANDSCAPES CAN change; use ChatGPT to stay updated on the legal terminologies or clauses that may have been updated or have become obsolete.

Tip 7: Automate Routine Communications

USE CHATGPT TO DRAFT routine legal communications like follow-ups or preliminary queries, freeing up your legal team's time for more complex tasks.

Tip 8: FAQ Generation

CHATGPT CAN HELP GENERATE a FAQ section for common legal queries related to the business, which can be a handy reference for both employees and investors.

Tip 9: Early Flagging of Red Flags

WHILE NOT A SUBSTITUTE for legal counsel, ChatGPT can assist in flagging potential issues that should be reviewed by your legal team.

Tip 10: Compile Legal Best Practices

USE CHATGPT TO COMPILE a list of best practices or guidelines for dealing with common legal scenarios, adding an educational component to your legal strategy.

Chapter 46: Drafting and Editing Grant Applications

Funding for startups isn't limited to venture capital or angel investors. Grants are a fantastic way to raise funds without giving away equity. However, the process is notoriously competitive and involves lengthy applications filled with technical jargon and complex requirements. ChatGPT can be your digital partner in this endeavor.

The Importance of Grants

- Equity Preservation: Grants provide funding without diluting your ownership.

- Validation: Winning a grant often serves as an endorsement of your idea, which can attract further investment.

- Resource Pool: Many grants come with mentorship, training, and networking opportunities.

How ChatGPT Can Aid You

Research: ChatGPT can help summarize requirements or guidelines for different grants, ensuring you apply for those that are most relevant.

Content Generation: From executive summaries to technical descriptions, ChatGPT can help draft sections of the grant application, which can later be fine-tuned.

Proofreading: Before submitting, ChatGPT can provide a final review for grammar or stylistic errors that might have slipped through the cracks.

Real-world Scenario

IMAGINE YOUR ED-TECH startup aims to improve literacy rates in underprivileged areas.

Without ChatGPT: You might spend weeks sifting through grant opportunities and then rush to complete the application, possibly missing key points.

With ChatGPT: You get a compiled list of suitable grants and a well-structured first draft, giving you ample time for revisions and increasing your odds of success.

Navigating the complex and often tedious process of drafting and editing grant applications can be a significant hurdle for startups and businesses looking for funding. ChatGPT can serve as a valuable assistant during this process, helping you draft initial applications, edit existing ones, or even generate summaries and bullet points to help crystallize your project's objectives and value proposition.

Tip 1: Utilize Templates

CHATGPT CAN GENERATE basic grant application templates that are tailored to the requirements of specific granting organizations. Use these as a starting point for your applications.

Tip 2: Content Review

USE CHATGPT TO REVIEW the content for clarity, consistency, and relevance. A well-reviewed grant application significantly improves your chances of obtaining funding.

Tip 3: Summarizing Objectives and Goals

CHATGPT CAN HELP YOU articulate the objectives and goals of your project in a concise and impactful manner. This is vital for capturing the attention of grant review committees.

Tip 4: Generate a Project Timeline

LET CHATGPT GENERATE a preliminary timeline for your project, showcasing major milestones and projected outcomes. This adds credibility and thoroughness to your application.

Tip 5: Final Checks

BEFORE SUBMITTING THE grant application, use ChatGPT to perform a final review, checking for errors or inconsistencies that could undermine your application.

Chapter 47: Summarizing Regulatory Guidelines for Investment

———

Fundraising is not just about dazzling investors with your innovation and business acumen; it's also about compliance with various rules and regulations. Failure to adhere to these regulations can result in legal issues, penalties, or even the closure of your business. Let's discuss how ChatGPT can assist you in this essential area.

Why Regulatory Compliance Matters

● Investor Confidence: Compliance signals to investors that you know how to operate within the boundaries of the law.

● Legal Protection: A compliant startup is less likely to face legal troubles, saving you money and headaches in the long run.

● Global Expansion: Understanding and complying with regulations makes it easier to enter new markets.

How ChatGPT Can Help

Regulatory Summaries: ChatGPT can quickly summarize complex regulatory documents, highlighting the most crucial aspects you should focus on.

Checklists: ChatGPT can generate checklists based on regulatory guidelines to help ensure that you haven't missed any compliance steps.

Updates and Alerts: While it's not real-time, a regular check-in with ChatGPT can keep you informed of regulatory changes that might affect your business.

Real-world Application

IMAGINE YOU'RE RUNNING a telehealth startup.

Without ChatGPT: You might have to rely solely on legal advisors for all compliance-related tasks, which can be expensive and time-consuming.

With ChatGPT: You can get a quick summary and checklist based on the latest telehealth regulations, thus arriving at meetings with your legal team better prepared and more informed.

The complexities of navigating regulatory frameworks should not be underestimated, especially when you're in the arena of attracting investments. With ChatGPT, not only can you make sense of these complexities, but you can also effectively communicate them to your stakeholders. The AI-powered tool helps you filter through legal noise to focus on what's important, ensuring you're investment-ready from a regulatory standpoint.

Tip 1: Prioritize Key Regulations

BEFORE DIVING INTO any regulatory text, consult with your legal team to identify the key regulations that are pertinent to your business. Use ChatGPT to summarize these specific sections for quicker assimilation by all team members.

Tip 2: Legal Liaison

USE CHATGPT TO CREATE easy-to-understand briefs that can be shared with your legal advisors for review. It streamlines the communication between your startup team and legal professionals, saving time and reducing the likelihood of misunderstandings.

Tip 3: Regular Updates

USE THE AI TOOL TO schedule regular updates on any changes or amendments to regulatory guidelines. This keeps your summaries up-to-date and ensures ongoing compliance.

Tip 4: Internal Training

COMPILE THE AI-GENERATED summaries into training material for your team. ChatGPT can help create quizzes or knowledge checks to ensure everyone understands the regulatory obligations.

Tip 5: Investor Relations

COMPILE A SIMPLIFIED guide on the most important regulatory aspects concerning your business. Share this guide with potential investors to demonstrate your commitment to compliance and governance.

Chapter 48: Scripting "How It Works" Video for Investor Pitch

———

I n a world dominated by visual content, a well-crafted "How It Works" video can provide a significant advantage when wooing investors. A good video not only explains your product but also conveys your brand personality. Here's how ChatGPT can contribute to making your pitch unforgettable.

The Power of Visual Storytelling

- Instant Clarity: A well-executed video can explain complex ideas quickly, providing instant clarity to prospective investors.

- Emotional Connection: Videos can tap into emotions more efficiently than text, enhancing the overall impact of your pitch.

- Branding: A unique video style can set you apart from competitors.

How ChatGPT Can Assist

Scripting: ChatGPT can help draft an engaging and clear script that outlines your product's features and benefits, as well as the problem it solves.

Storyboard Ideas: Although ChatGPT can't draw, it can suggest scenes or visual elements to include in your video.

Tips and Best Practices: ChatGPT can offer advice on pacing, tone, and essential elements to include for a compelling investor-focused video.

Real-world Use Case

LET'S SAY YOU'VE DEVELOPED an AI-based personal fitness coach.

Without ChatGPT: You may spend hours jotting down ideas, editing, and second-guessing every line in your script, thus delaying production.

With ChatGPT: You start with a well-structured draft that captures the essence of your product, shortening the production timeline and refining your storytelling.

In an investor pitch, showing is often better than telling. A well-crafted 'How It Works' video can breathe life into your business concept, making it easy for investors to grasp your value proposition and business model. ChatGPT proves to be an invaluable asset in scripting such videos, enabling you to focus on delivering a compelling visual narrative that captures the essence of your business.

Tip 1: Start with an Outline

BEFORE RUNNING THE script through ChatGPT, create a rough outline covering the key points you want to convey in the video. This will give a structured direction to the AI and make sure all critical aspects are covered.

Tip 2: Test Run with a Sample Audience

ONCE THE SCRIPT IS generated, consider a test run by presenting it to a sample audience before the final shoot. Use ChatGPT to compile their feedback and make necessary script refinements.

Tip 3: Incorporate Numbers and Data

INJECT YOUR SCRIPT with relevant statistics or performance metrics that can bolster your business case. ChatGPT can help format these numbers in a way that is easy to understand and remember.

Tip 4: Address Possible Objections

USE CHATGPT TO SCRIPT sections that preemptively answer questions or address objections investors might have. This shows you're thorough and have considered multiple facets of your business.

Tip 5: Include a Call to Action

DON'T FORGET TO END your video with a strong call to action. ChatGPT can help you craft a persuasive closing line that encourages investors to take the next step in engaging with your business.

Chapter 49: Designing Investor Outreach Campaigns

———

Investor outreach is like dating—you've got to put yourself out there, make the first move, and stand out in a sea of potential matches. But unlike dating, you're looking for someone willing to invest time, faith, and money into your business dream. Here's how ChatGPT can help you woo your financial soulmate.

Why Investor Outreach Campaigns are Essential

- Visibility: Without outreach, even the best business ideas can go unnoticed.

- Credibility: A well-structured outreach campaign shows you're serious about your business venture.

- Feedback: Outreach isn't just about seeking funds; it's also a way to get valuable feedback from savvy industry insiders.

How ChatGPT Can Help

Content Strategy: ChatGPT can help you map out the types of content you'll need for your campaign, such as emails, blog posts, or social media updates.

Personalized Templates: Create customized outreach emails that resonate with different categories of investors.

Follow-up Suggestions: ChatGPT can generate a variety of follow-up messages, ensuring you're not sending the same "Just checking in" email ad nauseam.

Real-world Example

SUPPOSE YOU'VE FOUNDED a clean energy startup.

Without ChatGPT: You're manually crafting each outreach email and struggling with maintaining consistent and timely follow-ups.

With ChatGPT: You've got a suite of templates and a strategic follow-up schedule, freeing you up to focus on building relationships rather than writing emails.

Investor outreach is not merely a matter of sending bulk emails or making a few calls; it's about developing a targeted, engaging, and data-driven campaign that resonates with your potential stakeholders. ChatGPT simplifies this complex process by providing a myriad of ways to plan, execute, and analyze your outreach efforts, ensuring that your message reaches the right people at the right time and in the most effective manner.

Tip 1: Segment Your Investor List

CHATGPT CAN HELP YOU categorize your investors based on various factors like industry focus, investment size, or geographic location. This segmentation allows for more personalized and relevant outreach, increasing the chances of engagement.

Tip 2: Optimize Email Subject Lines

FIRST IMPRESSIONS MATTER. Use ChatGPT to craft compelling email subject lines that encourage the recipients to open your email, a crucial first step in any successful outreach campaign.

Tip 3: A/B Test Outreach Methods

DON'T PUT ALL YOUR eggs in one basket. Use ChatGPT to design multiple versions of your outreach materials. Then run small-scale tests to find out which version generates the best response, and scale that up.

Tip 4: Follow-up Smartly

TIMING IS EVERYTHING when it comes to follow-ups. Use ChatGPT to generate a follow-up schedule and script that keeps you on the radar of potential investors without becoming intrusive.

Tip 5: Analyze and Adapt

AFTER YOUR CAMPAIGN, utilize ChatGPT to sift through the data, summarizing key performance indicators and investor responses. Use this data to refine your future outreach strategies.

Chapter 50: Creating Agenda for Investor Meetings

An investor meeting is like a first date where you have to discuss prenuptial agreements. It's critical, it's nerve-wracking, and how well you prepare can make or break the relationship. A well-structured agenda is your roadmap to success, and ChatGPT can be your trusty GPS.

The Importance of a Solid Agenda

● Focus: An agenda keeps everyone on track, ensuring that key topics are covered.

● Time Management: Meetings can drift, but an agenda can be your anchor, keeping things succinct and productive.

● Professionalism: Walking into an investor meeting with a clear agenda demonstrates you mean business—literally.

How ChatGPT Can Assist

Drafting: ChatGPT can help you outline an agenda that covers all the essential points, from introduction to financials to Q&A.

Flexibility: Your ChatGPT-generated agenda can be easily modified to fit different types of investors or meeting formats.

Talking Points: The AI can generate bullet points or even a script for each item on the agenda to help you prepare.

Real-world Application

IMAGINE YOU'RE LAUNCHING a mental health app.

Without ChatGPT: You might fumble through the meeting, forgetting key points and wasting time on less crucial matters.

With ChatGPT: You walk into the meeting with a streamlined, comprehensive agenda that not only keeps you on track but also impresses your potential investors.

Preparing an agenda for investor meetings can seem like a daunting task. It requires a perfect blend of content and timing to ensure the meeting is productive. ChatGPT can be a game-changer in this context, helping you to design a focused and engaging agenda that ensures you cover all crucial points while leaving room for meaningful discussion. Employing this AI tool can be the difference between a successful investor meeting and a wasted opportunity.

Tip 1: Prioritize the Most Important Points

USE CHATGPT TO HELP you identify the most important topics that need to be covered in the meeting. Once they are identified, you can use the tool to help you structure the meeting agenda so that these points are addressed first.

Tip 2: Allocate Time Slots Wisely

WITH CHATGPT'S HELP, you can define time slots for each agenda item based on its complexity and importance. This ensures that you don't run over time, which is crucial when you're dealing with busy investors.

Tip 3: Include Interactive Elements

TO KEEP INVESTORS ENGAGED, it's useful to have some interactive elements in your agenda. ChatGPT can assist you in designing short quizzes or polls that can break up the meeting and keep everyone engaged.

Tip 4: Leave Room for Q&A

DON'T FORGET TO ALLOCATE a significant chunk of time for questions and answers. ChatGPT can help you predict possible questions that might be asked, allowing you to prepare your answers in advance.

Tip 5: Post-Meeting Follow-up

UTILIZE CHATGPT TO generate a follow-up email summarizing the meeting and outlining the next steps. It's a professional touch that shows you value your investors' time and involvement.

Chapter 51: Writing an Impact Report for Social Entrepreneurs

———

If regular entrepreneurs are artists, social entrepreneurs are muralists—they paint on the large canvas of society, aiming for impact beyond the balance sheet. And just like artists need to showcase their portfolio, social entrepreneurs must present Impact Reports. Think of these as your magnum opus that articulates your mission, your impact, and why investors should join you on this virtuous voyage.

Why Impact Reports Matter

- Trust: Investors need to know their money is creating measurable positive change.

- Visibility: An Impact Report shines a spotlight on your mission and achievements.

- Engagement: These reports aren't just for investors; they can energize your entire stakeholder ecosystem.

ChatGPT to the Rescue

Structure: Unsure what to include in your Impact Report? ChatGPT can help you outline the essential sections—from the executive summary to case studies.

Data Presentation: Converting your impact metrics into understandable narratives or even infographics is a cinch with ChatGPT.

Storytelling: Human stories captivate. Let ChatGPT help you weave compelling narratives around your data.

A Practical Example

SAY YOU'RE RUNNING a startup aimed at reducing food waste.

Without ChatGPT: You may struggle with how to present your yearly impact in a digestible way.

With ChatGPT: Not only do you have a well-structured report, but it's also filled with engaging stories and data points that effectively communicate your impact.

For social entrepreneurs, conveying the impact of their work isn't just a formality; it's a necessity. An impact report doesn't just measure financial returns; it also accounts for social and environmental gains. ChatGPT can play an invaluable role in crafting an impactful report that resonates with stakeholders, from investors to community members. Using this AI tool ensures that your report is not only compelling but also accurately reflects the depth and breadth of your venture's positive impact.

Tip 1: Focus on Storytelling

CHATGPT CAN HELP YOU weave your data and facts into a compelling narrative. People connect more with stories than with numbers alone, so use this storytelling approach to make your impact report more relatable and engaging.

Tip 2: Utilize Data Visualizations

INCORPORATE CHARTS, graphs, and other data visualizations in your report to make complex data easily understandable. ChatGPT can assist you in generating descriptive captions or even suggesting types of visualizations that can complement your text.

Tip 3: Highlight Case Studies

INDIVIDUAL STORIES or case studies can make your impact tangible. Use ChatGPT to draft these stories in a way that they underline your overall mission and the impact you're making.

Tip 4: Include Future Goals and Aspirations

WHILE AN IMPACT REPORT primarily focuses on the past, it should also look towards the future. ChatGPT can help you articulate your future plans in a way that aligns with what you have already achieved, setting the stage for ongoing impact.

Tip 5: Make it Shareable

ONCE YOUR REPORT IS ready, you'll want to get it into as many hands as possible. ChatGPT can assist in creating a summary or even social media snippets that you can use to share your impact report widely.

About the Author

British based although in my 20s spent far to much time in the US and partying in Monaco.

Worked on many web firsts but during the dotcom boom I got to be a founding part of Commerce One which was a Dotcom darling.

I then went bust, Commerce One went chapter 11 and I was 30. But when you have slept in bus shelters at the age of 18, you take everything in your stride.

Since then have built numerous companies, messed some up and have Pario Ventures which is me and my mates business with over 100 investments.

Why am I called The Grumpy Entrepreneur, we have my wife to thank for that. Her idea back in 2012 and since then I have trademarked it. Anyway enough of me, lets move on.

Feel free to drop me a message.

Twitter @thegrumpye

Linkedin - David Murray-Hundley The Grumpy Entrepreneur | LinkedIn

Read more at https://www.parioventures.com.

Milton Keynes UK
Ingram Content Group UK Ltd.
UKHW010931231123
433129UK00001B/113

9 798223 261735